OUR LIFE'S ADVENTUROUS JOURNEY

MICHAEL W. COTIE

STRATTON
—PRESS—
Publishing Life

Our Life's Adventurous Journey
Copyright © 2020 **Michael W. Cotie**

Stratton Press Publishing
831 N Tatnall Street Suite M #188,
Wilmington, DE 19801
www.stratton-press.com
1-888-323-7009

ISBN (Paperback): 978-1-64895-210-4
ISBN (Ebook): 978-1-64895-211-1

Printed in the United States of America

ACKNOWLEDGMENT

To my dearest darling Debbie, my love, my life, my all, I dedicate this book to you. The story of our lives both before marriage and continuing on. Through thick and thin, hard times and harder times, you have stuck it out. I love you with all my heart!

Your loving husband,
Michael

CONTENTS

INTRODUCTION

As we were driving the other day, Debra and I were discussing many things. The subject of my book *A Christian Father: A Man of Faith* came up. As we talked, we begin to talk of our lives together, and she suggested I write this book.

We have gone through many things in our forty-plus years of marriage. Through good times and bad times, as well as in between, we have honored our commitment to each other. Through the birth of our children and now our grandchildren, which have just been born. From tough financial times to times where we abounded. We have stuck out the marriage.

When many times, giving up seemed like a better option, we continued to work through all. Because giving up for Christians is never really an option. God places things in our lives to strengthen us to make us better Christians and better people. 1 Corinthians 10:13 states this, "There hath **no temptation taken** you but such as is common to man: but God is faithful, who will not suffer you to be tempted above that ye are able; but will with the temptation also make a way to escape, that ye may be able to bear it." As you learn to bear up under those things and not give in, you find the way of escape. Let me interject here the way of escape as I see it, is this, Prayer leads us to Faith that is a life of Resting in our Faith. Faith that God will accomplish all that He Promised in Philippians 4:19, "But my God shall supply all your need **according to his** riches in glory by Christ Jesus." And Romans 8:28, "And we know that all things work **together for** good to them that love God, to them who are the called according to his purpose." Finally practicing Ephesians 4:26, "Be ye angry, and sin not: let not the **sun go down** upon your wrath." A book we were given before marriage stated this, "Don't let the sun go down on your anger"; that is, don't let the things you argue about continue into the next day, get the anger out before you go to sleep. Sound solid advice for couples today.

From our first meeting to our finally coming together, things have been a whirlwind for us. But through it, God has seen us through. He brought us together and He will be with us till death us do part or the rapture occurs. Then we will be together with Him forever.

It is always a winning situation when God is on your side. Don't get me wrong, there have been many times we had differences, many times we have failed the Lord, but He has never failed to be with us. This is our story. A story of Love and Marriage, friendship and hardship, good times and bad. A marriage centered on service to God. With all the ups and downs of life. Come into the story of our lives as we continue to travel *Our Life's Adventurous Journey*.

CHAPTER 1

Debra's Life before Marriage

Debra and I have talked about this many times, and it still amazes us that we are together. Debra was born on a cold day in Buffalo, New York, in 1955. Her family lived there for the first four years of her life. Her dad, an ex-marine DI, had found employment with Bell Helicopter. He had been reared in Buffalo by very strict Christian parents.

Debra was actually born on Election Day that year. Her birth was a difficult one because she was a breech baby; this caused her navel to have problems. Her parents had to place a half dollar on the area and tape it to her, seems it tore somehow during the birth. The treatment worked, but during those early times, her dad had to calm her; he was the only one who could. From that incident, she became very close to her dad. She was a daddy's girl for sure.

Her older brother was just a little over one year older than her and then her sister came along fourteen months later. Followed by two more brothers, a family of five children. But they wouldn't be in Buffalo area forever. God had a plan for her, and a move would be necessary to accomplish His will. The baby brother actually being born in Texas.

Our Life's Adventurous Journey began thousands of miles apart and three months difference in our ages. God was at work in all this to ensure He brought right man and right woman together. You see, that is one key to a lasting marriage, seeking God for the right person. He will always work it out when you seek His will. Many would argue that point, but I truly believe He worked things out for our meeting and loving each other.

As I said, her dad was raised by strict Hard Shell Baptist parents. Debra told stories that he had shared with them. His family would go to church on Sunday, come home, and eat. Then he and his brother would have to go to bed and rest. Of course, he grew up as my dad did in the 1930–'40s America. Both in a time of depression and threats of war and actually World War II.

But as he grew into adulthood, the Korean War began, and he became a US Marine. As a young recruit, he was sent to Korea right into battle. A young Christian man in a bloody war. He would be wounded and receive double Purple Hearts. One wound was from a projectile entering through one side of his jaw and exiting on the opposite side. Yes, he survived! God was watching over him during that tumultuous time that is evident in his survival from that wound. He would say later he woke up with a terrible headache, and throughout his life, not one set of dentures fit him correctly.

Arriving back in the States, he was stationed in California, San Diego to be exact. He made a trip to North Carolina. While there, he met a young lady name Dollie. She would end up being the love of his life. He stayed on the beach a little too long on that trip, and his light skin caused a major sunburn. Anyone who has been in the military knows that this could cause a court-martial. You see, a soldier is the property of the United States and he had abused that property. Not only that, but he also had to hitch a ride back to California and then report; he was punished but not by court-martial. Almost being AWOL, I guess in his mind, Dollie was well worth it.

Upon receiving his honorable discharge from the Marine Corps, he married Dollie, the Southern belle from North Carolina; can you see the pattern here? God has a right person for everyone and circumstances are arranged for those who seek that right person God has for them, and they will find that right person. Good advice for Christian young people today: pray for God to give you the mate He has for you.

They married in Rocky Mount, North Carolina, on the steps of the courthouse that remains today. Shuffling off to Buffalo, a Southern girl in a Northern town. She had the Southern drawl and heard all about it from the local residents. With their first living child being born three years after their marriage. Then Debra would be the second living child. Two miscarriages occurred in their family.

By the time they had been married eight years, they had four living children. He would then find a job with a new government entity, the National Aeronautic and Space Administration, that is NASA for short. He was required to first move to Hampton, Virginia. And their Debra would start school. A year later, he was offered a chance to make another move. This time, to the newly opening NASA complex in Houston, Texas. Which is now known as the Johnson Space Center.

He told them to sign him up, and the family moved on from Virginia. Debra was now going on seven years old. Their dad had left them in Virginia while he went to Texas, like many had before him. He lived at the YMCA in the Houston Area. Searching for a house, he found one that had 3 bedrooms, 1 ¾ baths, and a two-car garage. It was in the city of Pasadena, Texas. The family was flown to Houston via military aircraft landing at Ellington Air Force Base. It would happen that about a year later, her baby brother was born, and their family was complete. Debra and I are now only about ten miles apart, but have not met and will not meet for quite a few more years.

Her dad also found a church for the children to attend and then he begin attending too. Becoming a deacon of the church and being a faithful believer. He ensured his family was brought up in a Christian environment and attending church regularly.

He would become the president of the local Little League, even helping design the playing facilities. Debra remembers being sent to the scoreboards to keep score. In those days, nothing was electronic. The numbers were large metal placards, and she and her sister would carry them up the steps to the scoreboard. Sitting and placing the correct numbers as scoring was occurring. All her brothers played ball on those fields, which was just a short walk from their home.

She tells about their time outside with friends, but when bedtime came, they had better be home and ready for bed. When it was 7:30 p.m., they had to be in bed. Her friends would come knocking on their window, wanting them to come out and play. They would tell them to go away, they would get in trouble. So every evening, they were in bed by 7:30 p.m.

When she was in the third grade, the doctors would find a cyst on her leg, and it needed to be removed. She was not able to attend school for several weeks, and her dad worked with her on her lessons. Her grades suffered due to this surgery. That was a tough school year for her. She couldn't walk on the leg for several weeks.

One year, she received a watch for a gift, and as she was ready to walk home from school, it had begun to rain. She put the new watch in her pocket to keep it from getting wet and causing it to stop working. When she arrived home, she placed her hand in the pocket and no watch, the pocket had a hole in it, and the watch had slipped out of that hole. She retraced her steps all the way to school about a mile and then back; as she approached their home, she spotted the watch on ground and was elated to have found that precious gift. They would play with the neighbors as much as they could, but bedtime would come and they would need to be home, in fact, they would be in when their dad arrived home from work and then no more going out. Chores would need to be completed as well as schoolwork. With only one bathroom, the five would have to work through taking their baths and getting ready for bed.

Debra recalls an incident with her younger brother who was told to eat everything on his plate. He sat for over an hour crying as he just couldn't finish his dinner. From that point on, her mom told her dad that they wouldn't be forced to eat their entire meal.

Debra and her sister had dishes to do, and they had to wait that evening for his plate. Debra's sister became quite a seamstress and made a dress; Debra recalls her sister sitting in the closet, hemming the dress, and then their mom taking it the next day after school and letting the hem out.

During her early life, the family would make several vacation trips to Buffalo, New York, or Rocky Mount, North Carolina, to visit grandparents. Her most memorable would be in her early teenage years. When they went to their paternal grandparents, the old cliché would apply: "Children are to be seen but not heard." They would have to sit and be quiet while the adults carried on a conversation. But her maternal grandparents' house was quite different. On many of the North Carolina trips, she recalls shelling purple hull peas and her fingers turning purple; she would then be told they were a part of her supper. Many times on those trips, her dad would be found at the barbecue pit, cooking for all of Debra's mom's family. Debra, her siblings, and cousins would be given some money to walk to the local store for soda waters and a candy bar. They would normally bring change back from a dollar. Their grandfather had to have his orange crush soda as a part of the deal. Then the homemade ice cream would be made, and they would fight over who would turn the crank or sit on the bucket.

One year, a banner year for NASA, her dad had a vacation planned, and it didn't quite work the way he planned it. Work required that he be there; they ask him to put off the vacation, and if he would, they would make it up to him, they would reward him greatly. An important space flight was to occur and all hands were needed; it was July of that year, probably the most important of all space flights was going to take place. July 21, 1969, the first man stepped foot on the moon. Having completed the mission, they could now take their vacation, and they allowed him to take five weeks. Their vacation was to Buffalo, New York, and then down to Rocky Mount, North Carolina, they made it to both grandparents' homes that year.

The trip to Buffalo was to be in celebration of his parents fiftieth wedding anniversary and his brother's twenty-fifth. The vacation was to be between the two; now they arrived a little late but had much more time to spend. This trip they were able to interact with their Northern cousins and able to play just a bit more. This trip, she was now becoming a young lady and had different things happening to her. The North Carolina trip was especially that way.

She recalls a picnic of some type whether family reunion or exactly the type is not clear in New York on this trip. A jar filled with buttons was passed around for all the kids to guess how many. Debra guessed the closest and won a small jar of strawberry jam. She still wins door prizes and things even today.

Her paternal grandparents would make it down to Texas the next year and that would be the last time she saw her paternal grandfather as he passed away the next year. Her maternal grandfather would pass a year or so after the visit that summer of 1969. Losing both grandfathers in a short span of time. Life continues and her life did.

As her maternal grandfather's health deteriorated, her mom was called and told to come as soon as was possible. A long trek to North Carolina, but somehow their dad came up with the money for an airline ticket. Debra's grandmother had been sitting up with her husband and would not leave his side. When his baby girl arrived, she was asked to get their mom to sleep and take care of her. She was able to get their mom from his bedside and get her to sleep. Everyone feels like her dad knew she was there, and thus, he passed early in the morning after her arrival.

Back home, Debra and her sister were called upon to cook dinner. They were going to have spaghetti, and as Debra was pouring the water off the cooked spaghetti, it spilled in the sink. The standing joke for a while was they had kitchen sink spaghetti. But all went well with Mom gone and the girls taking care of the house.

Later in that time, their neighbors, who lived across the street, invited them on a fishing trip to Toledo Bend Reservoir. They all went, and as Debra was walking down a steep concrete embankment, she slipped and hit her head hard on the concrete, dazing her for just a few moments. She never told her mom about this, and other than telling me, no one else has ever known. She said she was dizzy for a while and didn't feel good for few days. Most likely a concussion that went untreated.

As a young girl, she wanted desperately to learn to play the piano, and she and her dad went searching for a piano. They found one that they liked, but her dad decided not to purchase it. She also loved the choir in intermediate school, her dad even made her dress, but she dropped out because she felt her dad wouldn't be able to take her to the contest which was a mandatory requirement to be in choir. Many things she wanted to participate in but was afraid her dad would say no, so she decided not to even try.

Through her teenage years, she would have a few boyfriends and a few of those relationships were getting serious, probably just for her, when things occurred and they would split up. She even met one boyfriend at the baseball fields down the street from their home because she was afraid her dad would not approve. She was attending church and involved somewhat in her youth group. There were a few boys of interest, but she had about decided that she would never get married and just work all of her life, but God had different plans.

As she grew into her teenage years, they changed churches several times. Baptists seem to like to do that. Therefore, they attended several churches. After one church split, they ended up having church at the local YMCA building. Debra talks about her dad arriving early and helping to set up chairs, leading music, and even teaching Sunday school.

The church they attended at the YMCA closed its doors, and they would need to find another one to attend. A controversy had arisen concerning the boys and girls swimming together, and the church folded over that one issue.

Debra and her sister begin to cross the channel with their neighbor lady, who just happened to play the piano at the church I was attending. Now she is coming closer to me and the area in which I lived. They had begun attending with her, and the first night they came, a friend of mine was attracted to Debra's sister and was going to meet them. He said, "Come go with me," and shy me said no and I stayed in the place I always sat. Debra was now in high school.

All this time, she and I are living about ten miles apart with a channel separating us. A tunnel was utilized to travel back and forth and one bridge over the Houston Channel had been finished on the 610 loop.

We had a thriving youth group at the time and a Monday night Bible study was held in different families' homes. Her sister, now dating my friend, came to his house for one of those Bible studies, and Debra came and was sitting on the couch. I had a slight crush on her by then, but she wouldn't even look my way. She was sitting on the couch and I on the floor, close to her. She doesn't even remember me being there to this day.

We still hadn't become a couple, and the way things were going, it was never going to happen, that is not unless God intervened. He would need to somehow help me through my shyness and give me the courage I would need to ask her to go out with me. She would have to notice me too, and I was not her type from what I understand of her choices of guys.

Things stayed status quo for both of us for a year or so. Being around each other at church and Bible study, but neither one making a move to get a relationship going. She wasn't really even interested in me and hadn't even noticed me.

The only thing happening was I was praying for God to send me the right girl (woman). Debra wasn't seeking a boyfriend at all; she felt she was going to go to work all of her life and remain single. But as I said, God had different plans. She was involved in VOE at school and was working. She had no interest in finding someone and was like me, a little introverted. Things would need to be worked up in a big way for us to ever come together and for God's plans to come to fruition for us.

CHAPTER 2

Michael's Life before Marriage

As for me, I was born in a suburb of Houston, Texas. My dad was raised Catholic and had been saved in 1949 as seen in my book, *A Christian Father: A Man of Faith*. As I was growing up, we had a lot different lifestyle than that of Debra's, yet in many ways, they were similar. While Dad was a faithful Christian and we attended church regularly, my upbringing was entirely different. As were my parents compared to Debra's.

The suburb I was born in had its own small hospital that today is a nursing home. Mom was concerned about me being born in a leap year, and well as you know, that only occurs every four years; however, I was not born on the twenty-ninth of February to her relief. I was born three months and several days after Debra.

Dad, in my early days, never really had steady work. He worked in a steel mill and would be laid off for months at a time. Once he would get back to that job, there would be a strike, so finances were up and down.

I had an older brother and an older sister. As many know, the baby of the family is the brunt of the older children's wrath. That was me, always being picked on, even being what would be called bullied today by my brother. I look at it as sibling rivalry and big brother ensuring his space wasn't violated; to me, that is common in all families.

As early as I can remember, something was happening to me. In a home movie, my brother draws his toy revolver from its holster and hits me in eye, now that was an accident. I was climbing on a fifty-gallon drum to look inside and fell and hit my chin. But my brother and sister also did their fair share of things to me. My sister jokingly says today I deserved it.

My grandparents lived in the Houston area. Dad's mom lived in Northeast Houston and my mom's parents about three or four miles from our house. We would visit both families quite often. My uncles, Dad and Mom's brothers, would take my brother and me fishing quite often. On one trip with my dad's baby brother is memorable, we were fishing at Sheldon Reservoir and a lady did something with her car, and it ended up in the water all way to the top of the car. My family was quite closer to us, whereas Debra's family was thousands of miles from her.

We would go to Mom's parents and play on the empty lots next to their home. One day, as my sister and I were playing, I picked up a stick and threw. My sister looked down and yelled, "Snake!" I turned just long enough to see a copperhead and we ran to the house. My uncles had a four-wheel cart, the rear axle came off wheels and all and while my brother was trying to pull my sister on it. I was rolling them through the burn pile my Papaw used in those days. I would grab my brother's football and take off with it. We had some good times in those early years.

Our vacations consisted of one or the other grandparents travelling with us. We went to Colorado with Mom's parents one year. I was probably four or five and wanted to hang out with my uncles and brother, well, they were sitting around a campfire and I walked up wanting to sit down beside one of them. My mom's baby brother grabbed my shoulder and said sit by me. He pulled me down on a cactus, and of course, I let out a scream and began to cry. The tines entering me and the people we were visiting had to proceed to pull them out. One slow tedious process, and of course, I had trouble sitting for a few days.

On another trip, my sister picked up a rock at the place we were camping and threw it at me; my mouth was open and a perfect throw right into my mouth and hitting my tonsils. My brother always got into the action for a lot these things. One incident that is etched into me mentally and physically is the time he had a butter knife and heated it cherry red. I asked what are you going to do with that, and he grabbed my arm and said, "Brand you," which he did. I ran out of the house screaming as Mom and Dad were pulling up.

My dad coached my brother's Little League team for three years, just as Debra's dad was involved in Little League, and Dad had several team picnics, some things never change. The picnics are a little different today, but that has remained a constant here in Texas at least. I also played pee wee and minor league baseball but my passion was football.

I remember November of 1963 and the assassination of President Kennedy, my second grade year, Mrs. Callaway was my teacher. They brought a radio or broadcast the coverage over the speakers as things were unfolding. I remember telling Mrs. Callaway that my g-grandmother lived in Dallas, and I hoped the person didn't go into her house and harm her.

Fourth grade, I tried out for the sixth grade football team, yes, the schools had sixth grade football back then. I didn't make the team that year. Tried again in the fifth grade, but I was struggling with my grades so I quit. Dad asked me why and I told him, then progress reports came out. Not like today's progress reports, in our day, if you received one, you really didn't want it, it meant you were failing. Well, I received one and Dad understood why I had quit football. Several tragic events struck our family the next year.

I was walking home from school one afternoon of my sixth grade year, yes, we walked home from elementary, and the walk from elementary was probably five miles. Well, I was almost home when my aunt came driving up to pick me up. Dad had been at work spraying for rats and breathed in methyl bromide and he almost died. God was watching over him, as Dad would tell us; it seems a man who had been in a tragic accident on his motorcycle came into the emergency room at the same time and was pronounced dead. The doctors transferred that man's blood into Dad saving his life, yes, their blood types were alike.

A few months later, that year too my mom's cousin we called Uncle Oscar died in a car accident, this was right before Christmas. We made it through these tragedies. Dad would change jobs shortly after that incident and on his way to work would be in a collision; Dad stopped just short of hitting the person in front of him, but looked in his rearview and saw a truck approaching and fast. Dad said he turned the wheels to the right and held his foot to the brake. POW, a rear-end collision and our truck was damaged. Dad made a deal with the insurance company, pay him the value of the truck and give him salvage rights, they agreed and it was settled.

Several times, we would go to Lake Houston at Alexander Deussen Park for boat rides and fishing. Dad ensured we had family time together. Many a Saturday or Sunday afternoon we spent swimming, boating, or fishing at the lake or even a picnic. Dad even joined several families in the rental of a fishing cabin on Luce Bayou in the northeast corner of Lake Houston. My sister and I would swim while our brother fished off the piers.

My eighth grade year brought more tragedy. My brother drowned and a cousin was killed in Cambodia. All in a two-week period May and June of that year. Tragedy and death were a big part of my life. A man at our church was working in a chemical facility and was burned to death in a refinery fire. Another man in our neighborhood killed his wife and two other people she had been cheating on him. His daughter was in one of my classes. So I have seen tragedy in my life.

Life of course continues to occur. In the ninth grade, my coaches decided a move in position was best for the team. I had been playing fullback and linebacker; they wanted me to play on the offensive line. I didn't like the move, but my choices were limited. I made the transition. As we were practicing one day, I was holding a handheld blocking pad, and one of my teammates hit me in the arm with his knee. The next day, my arm was swollen twice its size and I couldn't bend it. That cost me my entire ninth grade season.

During our track season, I was the anchor for the mile relay team. The finishing ¼ mile now 400 meters. We were participating in our district meet and the final race was that very mile relay. As the runner of the third leg approached, we were leading the pack. We had a good 5-yard lead on the rest of the competition. As we went for the baton exchange, his spikes caught the back of my foot and the spike dug in; my spikes flew off my feet. Baton exchange was successful though. As I was running on a cinder track only in my socks, the others gained some ground until the 330-yard mark that is when I kicked in the after burners so to speak. As I made my kick, we gained ground and finished about 10 yards ahead of the other competition. Coach timed me at a 56.4 quarter, the best I had ever run. The next week, the four of us on our mile relay team were running for the high school team in the district meet.

As I entered high school, yes, tenth grade was high school for us, football was my passion, and I continued running track and was in the choir while still attending church. I was a shy guy, barely able to approach girls unless they were friends. In these early phases of my sophomore year as we were in two a day workout training, the starting right guard on the varsity suffered an injury which the coaches weren't sure if he would recover from before the season started. The coaches approached me about moving up from the junior varsity team and I talked to Dad and we agreed that I could play on the varsity team. When the starting right guard healed and came back the coaches kept me on the varsity. I finished high school as a three-year letterman.

Track was interesting as I clocked a 10.5 hundred yard dash in a track meet my personal best. The quarter mile was my best race, running it in the mid-50's, for a 185 pound guy that played offensive guard that was real good in our time.

In choir, we were working on a musical, *Lil Abner*, and I played "Lonesome Polecat, Indian Brave." My costume consisted of a pair of gym shorts with flaps sown to the front and back. Our head football coach said that Indian had the largest thighs he'd ever seen, I was very muscular at the time. Agile and could run fairly fast, very athletic but very shy, and I have found out many called me the gentle giant, although I am only 5'10".

My junior year they moved me to right tackle, and I was the pulling tackle on sweeps and trap plays. We had a bad season winning only three games. Then my senior year came along and a move back to right guard and a pulling guard at that. That season, we had a great turn around with a winning season going 6-3-1 third in district play though.

One game that comes to mind was against a team who had beaten the year before. They had a long sustained drive at the end of the first half we were winning I believe 10–0 and they had driven the ball to the 3-yard line, goal line defense the coaches called as the 2-minute warning came to a close. I was over the right guard, and as the ball was snapped, I placed a forearm shiver on the guard and made the tackle, now second down, and their large 200+ pound full back in the game like the first play, guard fires out to block me a four arm shiver and I meet this guy in the back field as he is handed the ball. He went down in a heap as I pop up and see our line coach jumping up and down. Later, the guy next to me would say he was waiting to see who got up first from that hit. My dad was sitting about halfway up in the stands on the 50-yard line and he would tell me he heard that hit. The opposing team decided to run the ball to the opposite side, but as soon as the back felt a hit coming, he fell to the ground; we had a goal line stand at the end of the first half and went on to win that game.

I suffered a back injury in a game after that one and missed a week of practice, so I was allowed to suit up for homecoming but didn't get to play in that game. The next week, we played the district champs. Our star running back fell out of the back of a pickup truck on Halloween night and had to have twenty-seven stitches in his head. He didn't practice all week but was fitted with a piece of foam rubber and played the game. We lost that game and the offense never got on track that night.

Final game of my senior year, we were playing our biggest rival. They had defeated us two years in a row, and we wanted to defeat them for our senior year. It was a hard-fought game. We punted late in the game and their punt returner caught the punt started to run reverse field and one of our guys tackled him in their end zone for a safety. We received the kickoff and ran the clock out final score 2–0.

When it came to dating though it was very limited. Probably six dates throughout high school. A few reason, first I was shy when it came to girls; second, I thought I was too ugly for any girl to want me; and third, my brother's girlfriend had hurt Mom and Dad really badly and I didn't want them going through that after his death. There were many girls that I liked or had a crush on, but I simply would not get the courage to talk to them or ask them out.

One girl that I dated more than once and we were doing fairly well was in my junior year, but the relationship eventually stopped. Then there were several girls at church I had crushes on, but again too shy to even ask. One girl I had ask out was to go with me to the Springs Sports Banquet backed out on me during my senior year, and I asked a girl from school, a sophomore to go with me. But nothing lasting. Prom came, and well, a girl who was a good friend of mine agreed to go to prom just as friends.

A single college coach came recruiting and I went for a visit. The school had a nice campus and the team seemed to be a fairly successful one. Then I received the financial assessment of that school, it entailed several grants and loans per year. Too much, I felt for Mom and Dad to pay and I didn't want to be burdened with them, so I informed the head coach I wasn't coming there to play for them after all. Now I had no college plans going into the summer after my graduation.

My aunt and uncle had moved to Arkansas in the southernmost area. One weekend I helped my uncle move my grandparents into the house with them and went to visit the college in the next town. The coach invited to come back and start two a days in August. I went and found the admission office and ask for the admittance forms. I went home, talked to Dad, and sent off my application. They accepted me, and off to college in August, it would be. In the meantime, I was working a summer job attending church and Bible studies. Debra was at many of these Bible studies, but I still haven't gotten the courage to talk to her, much less ask her to go out with me.

CHAPTER 3
Finding Each Other

Well, as God would have it after going up and talking to the coaches and getting things set in motion God threw a curve, at least it would seem like it. His plan all the time we just don't know when He will answer prayer in most cases. You see, throughout high school every time I would get a crush or date a girl, I would pray, "If she is not the one you want for me, Lord, then show me." Something always occurred to show me she wasn't right.

I had been praying throughout high school for the girl He had for me. Shortly after getting home from Arkansas, I was back in church, and we were in the choir loft for choir practice. I looked down on the first row to see a girl I had a crush on and she smiled directly at me. Or at least I thought so. She says it wasn't directed to me, but I saw it that way. Well, that gave me courage, well probably, God the Holy Spirit gave me the courage when it comes right down to it. I went, picked up my Bible from the seat in the auditorium where I had planned to sit, and walked right up to her and asked if I could sit by her. The rest as they say is history!

After church, our youth group went to the local burger joint and I asked if she could go. We had to get permission from her mom and she said that she could go; we rode to the burger joint in my car. I asked her out on a date and she rode home with her sister and her sister's boyfriend. We talked on the phone during the week and I was given directions to her home. That next weekend, we went to the movies and watched what she wanted to see, *The Way We Were*. Saturday my family had my grandmother and grandfather's fiftieth wedding anniversary, Debra attended with me and then we left and went to my house, the church youth directors had a going-away party planned for me. We had a good time, and she had won my heart already.

I attended the service the next day, and then on Monday, I left for Arkansas. My cousins had been dropped off at their grandmother's in Corrigan and I stopped there to pick them up. We were off to Arkansas. I was coming into Nacogdoches when the trailer I was towing begin to push the vehicle forward and a state trooper stopped me and I was ticketed for ten miles over the speed limit. Upon arriving in Arkansas, I placed a call and found out how much I would need to pay and the hours of operation. I decided to go and pay it that weekend, and that also gave me an excuse to go home one last time before two a days started.

I went back and paid the ticket, then drove home for the weekend. Debra and I had another date and attended church together. Then off to Arkansas for college and football. She gave me her address, and we begin sending letters back and forth each week as I could. The weeks of two a days prevented me from staying at my aunt and uncle's house and I was very uncomfortable with that situation. But made it through then registered for my classes at the end of two a days. I was able to move back to my aunt and uncle's with all that good home cooking. Coach had tried to talk me into staying on campus and living. I was offered a full scholarship for football, but since I had to live on campus, I turned it down.

As college got into full swing for me and football going strong, I begin writing Debra and sent her my football schedule. The first game was to be played in Shreveport and Mom, Dad, and Debra came. It was raining hard and the field was a mess, but we won the game. They spent the weekend we had a short night and partial day visit. The second game was in Texarkana and Mom and Dad made that one and Debra wasn't able to come. Debra's dad had a heart attack and required triple bypass surgery. As he recovered in the hospital, she wanted to come to the homecoming game and asked for permission to which her father said she could that there was nothing she could do sitting at home. She came for homecoming; after the game, we drove to Texarkana to a steak house and was able to spend the weekend at my aunt and uncle's.

We continued growing and becoming closer. I ask her to marry me one of that weekends she came and plans were for her to come on her birthday weekend for the game. I went and bought a wedding set for her. On the night of her birthday, I gave her a t-shirt with my number on it and then the engagement ring. When they arrived home in the Houston area, she was sitting at the table helping her mother make the sandwiches for everyone's lunch when her mother looked and saw something sparkling on her ring finger. Her mom said what is that, and Debra showed her and said we are engaged.

The final game came, and I was able to correspond more with her even sending her my grade sheet. We discussed getting married at the semester break for both of us as she was in her senior year in high school but decided that the summer would be fine. She would graduate and then we could get married. As the first semester ended, I came home for the break and went to work at my old job from my junior year in high school. I worked on a garbage truck performing back door pickup. The job put more funds into my bank account for school. I had a scholarship waiting for me as Coach could now offered one and I could live off campus during non-football time. So Debra and I were able to be together for Christmas.

My grandparents had come down during that time and spent time with family they were to ride back with me to Arkansas. The day we planned to leave, it snowed in that area and roads were closed. We left the next day and stopped off to see my uncle who was now working in East Texas. Then on to Arkansas. I missed Debra but had gotten into my studies and working hard to pass my courses. Then February and spring football. As we started the spring workouts, another cold snowy day came. I was running a fever and not feeling well. I went to the school infirmary and the nurse told me not to get too overheated. Well, I informed the coaches who had moved workouts into the dressing room areas and they chewed me out for being sick. One said I messed up their whole workout schedule, the other said leave him alone, he just doesn't care.

The weekend before I had gone home, and as I was driving back from that visit after church on Sunday night, as I drove, I felt the Lord calling me into the ministry. That coupled with the coaches chewing me out me make a decision and I called Debra. The next day when the head coach came back from a recruiting run, I informed him that I would no longer play football. I called Debra later, we discussed it all and I decided to leave school. The only reason I was there anyway was for football. I was feeling even more God's call upon my life for ministry and knew I wouldn't get a Bible degree from this school. I went and checked out then called Mom and Dad and let them know. They of course were disappointed, but it was the best thing for me to do even in retrospect. I loaded my things and left for home.

Dad informed me I would need to find a job and so I begin my search that week. On a Saturday, I was over at Debra's and we were working on my friend's car who was dating Debra's sister. Their neighbor came over, and we began to talk; he needed a helper on the job he was on and offered me the job. Monday, I went to work in construction which has been my main career for over forty years. From that time forward, I have been in the business and the money was good, and eventually, I would have health coverage.

Debra and I saw each other on Wednesday nights for church as I would go and pick her up. Then I spent weekends during the day at her house when she wasn't working. We were growing closer and closer to each other in that time. We discussed how many children we would have if a boy and girl or vice versa were born first, we would only have two, but if we had two of the same sex, we would have a third. She would stay home and care for the kids and I would work as best I could. The kids having a stable home life similar to ours was more important than having things in our lives.

As May approached and my bank account increased, we were planning the wedding and working on finding furniture and an apartment. We stored the furniture and things we were buying at either my parents' house or her parents' home.

Then we decided on an apartment, a two-bedroom, I needed one room for my pool table. With the money I was making and the money now in the bank our finances were looking fairly good. On top of that, her high school graduation was fast approaching. Then two weeks later would be the wedding. We discussed my feeling of being called to ministry and she really didn't like the idea. I didn't surrender to His call at that time, as I said I needed to stay under our pastor's teaching a little longer then I will be ready.

Well, graduation came and it was raining. The school district would hold graduation indoors that would mean each student would only have a certain amount of tickets for family or friends. Well, her dad insisted, I go instead of him and I told him it was his place to go for his daughter. Well, he won out and stayed home getting her party ready. Graduation went off without a hitch the next step was the wedding for us.

We had signed the lease for the apartments and could move things in the first of June. We begin moving the furniture in and getting things in place, but neither of us would live there until after the wedding. I wanted to move in myself, but she would have no part of me in the apartment by myself this was going to be ours together. She won out on that one, and it was empty the first two weeks of that month. As we were leaving the apartment one evening, I was backing out of the parking space looking back. I forgot about the pole that supported the carport, cutting my wheels, I turned the right front fender into the pole and damaged the fender. Then a day or two later, we were moving and her brothers were helping, well, it started to rain hard. The street flooded and we were all flooded in. We walked to a small convenience store and bought a few snacks until her dad came in his station wagon and brought us home. My dad wanted to come get me since I shouldn't be spending the night at her home. But her dad assured him that everything would be fine so I spent the night on the couch and next day went and retrieved my car. Our furniture finally all moved in and some clothes along with my pool table all was set and ready for us to begin Our Journey through Faith.

CHAPTER 4

Our Journey Together Begins

Friday night, we all gathered at church for the rehearsal. Followed by the rehearsal dinner, Mom made her fried chicken and all the trimmings. I had ask my uncle who was seven years older than me to be my best man. I think I disappointed Dad, but he never really said anything.

Our wedding day finally arrived on a Saturday. Debra said her mom made her get up for an early start in completing task before the 7:00 p.m. wedding. Flowers were to be picked up. Then there were the cakes and decorations. Debra's dress would need to be loaded and everything taken to church. I called in the middle of everything, and we briefly spoke with each other.

Then the 7:00 p.m. time to begin came. The wedding vows were taken and we were married. Reception following and we went to our apartment together. Next morning, we got up dressed and made church. "OUR ADVENTUROUS JOURNEY" had begun with us in church the day after our wedding.

I worked all week, and on Friday afternoon when I arrived home, we left for a trip to Dallas. Took in Six Flags and spent time together. Had dinner and all together a great time. We travelled in her car because it had air conditioning. Then we arrived home Sunday night and life began together.

The first year we spent with ups and downs, but nothing really major occurred in our lives. I had advanced from helper to journeyman and a substantial raise. We made a few trips, and when the first year was over, I purchased a pickup truck. It was relatively new, and we kept Debra's car and traded mine in. Now I had my first pickup truck and Debra would buy me a camper shell for it a little later.

Debra had a friend in the apartment complex that gave her a dog, we named him Harvey, our first pet together. He was a German shepherd and ridgeback mix. He became a medium-sized dog. She loved Harvey and we were able to house break him. Now we had a companion for her in the daytime. In the evening, we spent time together watch TV on the black and white set, even played pool together on my table.

Debra's dad became the church softball team's coach and I started playing slow pitch softball with the team. Her older brother and second brother played and the baby brother was batboy. Debra's sister fiancé and eventual husband was on the team and his brother-in-law played on the team. The pastor's son-in-law and nephew played. There were several others who were kin in several ways, and we virtually had a family team, a church family, and physical family. Debra was given a job too; she became the score keeper. She enjoyed keeping score, and we were doing things together. Spending time and enjoying our new journey.

We began a search for a place we could call our own. We first looked at mobile homes and then a friend told us that a house would be a better investment and the search for a house began. First looking at new ones then we found a quaint little three-bedroom on blocks and piers. Purchased it and moved in. I was still on the same construction job at the time. We made our first move from an apartment to the house and now we were home owners. Things were still going fairly well for us. As our journey was really just starting, we reached our second anniversary and took a trip to San Antonio. We took in the Alamo and my favorite restaurant, a steakhouse we enjoy going to even today.

Debra and her mom took a trip to North Carolina to visit her grandmother. Her grandmother had been diagnosed with cancer and had also been in a car accident; she was in the hospital not doing well. They were gone nearly two weeks; this was the first time we had been separated since we were married and it was a long two weeks. We missed each other but spoke on the phone every night.

Debra and her mom arrived home and I picked her up at the airport; we got home and she unpacked. I had a softball game that afternoon and we made it to the game. I had been having allergy problems since high school and was getting worse. Missing time from work and just overall feeling bad. But I made the game and then home.

As life goes, she found out she was pregnant, and now we began to make plans for a new little one in our life. Well, as things progressed with her pregnancy, the project I had been working on was drawing to completion and I was laid off. House note, truck note, and a baby coming. But we decided to drive to North Carolina for a vacation before I began a search for a new job. We had money in the bank, and financially, we were doing well. Since her car didn't run well and my truck used a lot of gasoline, we borrowed Mom and Dad's car to make the trip. Her grandmother was back in the hospital, but we spent time with her aunt and uncle and met most of her family there.

As we drove, I would tell her stories of my growing up. As we were going through Louisiana, I recalled the time Mom had driven my dad's mother and sister-in-law to a funeral in Mississippi. My grandmother's brother had passed away. I told her how on the return trip the car started acting up and how I had Dad's tools and a quick removal of the gas filter had the car running better. Mom had always talked about how big of an eater I was. Well, we stopped at a seafood restaurant in Lake Charles, Louisiana. And I ordered a seafood platter. My grandmother and aunt said there's no way he can eat that much food, but I did and Mom's story of how much I could eat were now believed.

As Debra and I stopped for the night in Slidell to eat and get motel room, Debra got extremely sick to her stomach. A call to the doctor next morning and he said crackers and Sprite, travelling would be all right. We checked out of the motel and headed west. We arrived home later that afternoon and I got her settled into bed. By now, was starting to feel better.

I began my job search and found a job. For a little while at least. That one ended and I found another. We would take walks during the evening and discussed names. We talked about this name for a girl or that name for a boy. In those days, the ultrasound wasn't a routine thing, it was a choice. We decided to be surprised and so we just decided on names: one girl and one boy. We discussed family names as well as popular names. She didn't want a junior for the boy and we both tried to decide on names that could have no nickname attached. Finally settling on the girl's and boy's name.

We still had Harvey and had to put up a fence, but he was still getting out. We would have to search for him all over the neighborhood. As she got closer to having the baby and I had to go to work in Lufkin, we carried Harvey to the SPCA and left him. We were both sad to see him go, but it was for the best.

Now staying with my grandmother and grandfather in Corrigan my uncle who had lived in Arkansas would pick me up and take me to work with him. One day as we were working a seven-day, twelve-hour shift, I was instructed to clean the pipe with Varsol and so I walked up to an elderly man who didn't get along with most people and really I was about the only one who got along okay with him, I ask him if he had any Varsol I could borrow. To which he said I don't have anything you can borrow, I don't have anything anybody can borrow and he swung his 24" pipe wrench hitting me in the head. I shook my head and saw the blood dropping to the floor. The foreman rushed to my side and handed me a handkerchief by the time we walked downstairs and out the building it was covered with blood. It took fifty-seven stitches to sew me up as I arrived back on the jobsite there was my uncle, Big Don they called him, pacing, and they had called my aunt to come and pick me up. Well, she picked me up and drove me to my grandmother's place. She went in and told Debra to sit down and then told her what had happened then I walked in a gruesome sight. Eye swollen, black and blue. Debra being five months pregnant, we felt didn't need me to rush right in and we didn't want anything to happen with the baby. I was told not to come to work that next day and was paid to stay home. I had to go file charges on the man, but he checked back into the Rusk Mental Hospital in Rusk, Texas. I went to the dentist and had some teeth shaped up. Then back to work the next day and just light duty. Guys told me if they had hit me with a 24" pipe wrench and I didn't hit the ground, they wouldn't have stood there like he did. But I healed, and eventually, the job ended.

I found another shortly and went back to work now back home. First with the company, I had worked for when the man hit me, then back to my original company. Working on a new construction project. We were getting closer and closer to the time for our baby to be born. Thanksgiving and Christmas were coming. Dad had bought some property in Calvert, Texas, by this time and we made a few trips with him and mom to work on the place. It was cold and there was only an outhouse and a small electric heater. Debra got really cold on that trip. Dad was getting up to do some work early that morning and slipped his foot in his boot, well, there just happened to be a scorpion in one of the boots. And that boot came flying off his foot rather quickly.

On another trip, my uncle from Corrigan had come to help work on the tractor's hydraulics and just never could seem to get the problem solved. I did a little hunting on that trip and had been shooting at some birds, as I shot the birds fell and my uncle said that was a great shot, leading those birds. Well, we had squirrel and black bird breast for dinner that night.

CHAPTER 5
A Steeper Climb New Life

January 1978 came and so too was the time for a baby to arrive. The boy's and girl's names had been decided upon and the due date was fast approaching. I was working on a job about twenty miles from the house and expectantly waiting on a call.

Well, the due date came and went still no baby. Debra had a scheduled doctor's appointment. The doctor informed her that if she didn't start labor by the following Tuesday, then he would induce labor. Well, the weekend came and went and still not labor began. Tuesday came and we arrived early at the hospital in Pasadena, Texas. The doctor began the process of starting labor and as it began the pains of childbirth for Debra came. The induced labor began about 7:00 a.m. It was getting close to 1:00 p.m. and Debra said she had pressure feeling like she needed a restroom visit. But that wasn't the case, the baby was pressing and ready to be delivered. I was sent to the waiting room, and shortly the doctor came in and announced we had a boy. Our son came into this world, and we thought all was fine with him.

Well, it rained a lot that week and every day about 10:00 a.m. I would come in the room for a visit. Keep in mind, back in those days, the baby wasn't allowed in the room except at feeding time and even Daddy would be told to leave. Things are a whole lot different these days. About the third day it was time to take her and him home. Her dad let us use his car since my truck was higher and we arrived home safely with our little boy. Twenty-one inches long, six pounds, fifteen ounces.

Debra now settled in for life as a homemaker and me working. Well, I had been laid off from work again and was seeking a job. Which I found and went to back work. Our son was growing and became fussy so to get him to sleep we would drive him around at night. He was teething and we went to my mom's aunt's house and she gave us a small bottle of whiskey. A little on the fingertip and he settled down. She said, now don't tell anyone; well, she has passed away now and it is okay to tell that.

My allergies were still bothering me and I was missing time. The assistant pipe superintendent at the time called me in his office and told me to take a week and get to an allergist to find out what I was allergic to. A battery of test revealed the allergens that were causing the problems. I was allergic to mold, pollen, and house dust which really wouldn't be causing the nausea and swelling. But then the food allergens were a plethora of items. Corn, cucumbers, squash, okra, wheat, and honey. I began reading labels, many foods have corn sweeteners, corn oil, corn starch, and many other things made from corn. Then wheat is in many foods too. I found two soft drinks that had weird ingredients, one had ester of wood resin and another had polyethylene glycol.

I also had to give myself allergy shots and still had problems so I lost yet another job. I was able to go to work shortly and we decided to sell the little house. I was working in Baytown, Texas. We sold our house and moved into an apartment in Baytown, Texas. We had purchased a newer vehicle and finally were out of Debra's old clunker. I sold my pickup to Dad, and we had only one vehicle now. I rode my bicycle to the job and still had allergy problems but was able to work that job for over a year.

This was during the time of the gas crisis. Where you could only fill up on alternate days depending on your license number ending. We were still attending the church that we had met and married in, and I had lost the desire to pastor in some ways, but still felt the call in others.

We are now in an apartment, and I am still battling allergies. A layoff from that job as it came to an end, and I found another one and kept working as best I could. This job was in Alvin, Texas. Mom and Dad now in an apartment in Alvin, and we moved into an apartment in Pasadena, Texas. They had sold the house I grew up in, and now the farm would eventually be home base for them.

They sold the one place in Calvert and bought the property across the road which had a larger building but still an outhouse. There were fifty-three acres associated with this place though. It had a windmill well that wasn't working at the time. A five hundred-gallon tank upon a derrick that was rusted as I tell about in the book *A Christian Father, A Man of Faith.*

I received an ROF from the job in Alvin and had started working shutdowns that is where the plant is shut down for major renovations of operating materials, pipe, instruments, and the like. This involved working a seven-day, twelve-hour-plus shift normally for less than a month. Money of course was good but it was hard work. One evening, we had to work past the twelve-hour shift to empty catalyst from a vessel. I arrived home at midnight covered with black powder from head to toe. Debra put my clothes in the tub to get the black powdery substance and the stain was in that tub for quite a few months.

I had been sending letters out to pro-football teams about that time since my graduating class had graduated. Well, I received an invitation to come to training camp with the Dallas Cowboys. I had been staying in shape and was still very athletic still at that time. But I had a child and a wife. There was no pay at that time for attending training camp, and I needed to provide for my family. I decided not to take advantage of that opportunity.

I worked several shutdowns during this period of time; a shutdown is a time when a refinery or similar facility stops production for maintenance and repairs. I performed this with several companies and was making good money. About two years passed and I was working a good job behind a desk. Things seemed to be going well.

About that time, we found out Debra was pregnant again. We didn't want to be living in a two-bedroom apartment with a new baby coming and begin to look for a place of our own.

This time, we decided on a mobile home. It was an older model that had been refurbished and was not overly expensive. We made a deal and put money down on it. I began to search for a mobile home park we could park it in. Well, I finally found one in Channelview, Texas. Time came for the delivery of the trailer. Everything connected and in working order for us to move in sufficiently. Debra was over cleaning one morning. I had dropped her and our son off and went to work. Well, she became overheated and passed out for a short time. Finally regaining consciousness, she went outside under a shade tree and cooled down. We were finally able to have the A/C unit connected and cooling down the trailer. Settled in and things were going fairly well for us. Except I had nearly forgotten God's call upon me to preach.

I was now working every day, my allergies had cycled out, and my being inside may have helped in that too. This job seemed like the work was going to be steady. Shortly after moving in, our son was riding a Hot Wheels type toy and rode up under a van's fender as a lady was pulling into her driveway. I received a call at work from Debra and hurried to the hospital. X-rays revealed a broken foot and he would be required to wear a cast on that foot. He would not be able to walk for several months. We went to a company picnic with him in a cast, and I pulled him around in his little red wagon. It was hard to keep a 3 ½ year old down, believe you me. Our daughter was born in September of that year, and we now felt our family was complete. The trailer was settled into and we were doing well.

One evening while Debra was away and I was caring for the children, a fairly large needle we used for opening the nipples on the baby bottles had fallen on the floor. It was in the kitchen carpet and I came up to the counter with no shoes on my feet, I found the needle, it entered the ball of my foot. Then snapped off in my foot. With Debra gone, I called her brother-in-law to come to the trailer. He stayed with the children as I went to the emergency room. Debra finally arrived at the hospital and her brother-in-law left for home in his truck. This was in a severely cold time of year for the Houston area, and this doctor couldn't seem to get the needle out, so off we went to another hospital. This doctor made several incisions and out came the needle. I recuperated well from that little incident, but occasionally, I have scar tissue come off that foot.

During this time, we made several trips to the farm to help Dad and his time at Alvin had come to a close. He worked a small job in Baytown, Texas. They had purchased an old Spartan Park Type mobile home and moved into a trailer park in Channelview, Texas. Dad had been able to acquire a building from the construction site for just $1500. It was 20 × 30 and he had it moved in behind the current 12 × 20 building that existed when he purchased the "farm." We blocked and peered it and bolted it together as it came in two pieces. Then the arduous task of making it into a home. The whole family joined in on the effort to complete the house. My brother-in-law at that time was a carpenter; he and Dad and I all worked to get this building set. On our way home that weekend, I had a flat tire and eventually needed to replace the set. I had forgotten about God having called me to the ministry and we had settled in at church and home.

About that time, I had moved into a new office with a new project and this job fit me well. All inside work performing material take-offs. We decided it was time for a newer vehicle as the one we had was a two-door coupe instead of a four-door sedan. I found one that we felt would met our needs and made the trade with a little higher payment. Our daughter had just turned a year old and we were settling into life together. Still attending church and I was still sitting under our pastor as I had said I needed to do for a few years after quitting football and college. But soon, God began to deal with me.

The company I was working for had never in its history laid off mass amounts of people in their home office. It happened though, and I ended up unemployed. A search for a construction job proved futile. It was 1982 and the economic situation in the US was bleak especially in heavy industrial construction. The few construction jobs in the area weren't with the company I had been with and only those who were known were being hired.

A young lady at church was working for some people helping care for their animals. The man owned a refrigeration company and was looking for workers. The pay was quite a bit less than I had been making, but I needed a job and went to work for him. He gave me a company truck to drive back and forth to work. We ended up having our vehicle repossessed, and Dad gave us the Green Bomb back.

Since the man was providing me transportation to and from the job, he didn't pay me time and half for overtime. Which by the way was legal according to the labor board. I was working sixty to seventy hours a week and off mostly on Sundays. We had financial problems for another time in our marriage, this time not because of not working but because of the pay grade. God was of course dealing with me in all this about surrendering my life to the ministry. With all the hours I was working, Debra and I didn't see each other much, but we were still working through everything. I would call on a pay phone at lunch time to see how her day was going, something I still do even today.

Then late that year in October, the work for the refrigeration company stopped. Another layoff from work. I went to file for unemployment compensation and came home to a phone call. The mortgage company calling, demanding we catch up on the payments. I responded that I had just been laid off and wouldn't have any funds from unemployment for at least two weeks. I was told they would repossess the trailer and told them we would be out in two weeks.

Debra asked her parents if we could live with them for a while and we were told no. I called Dad and ask if we could move to the farm. He answered in the affirmative and we began to make plans to move. I went to farm and pulled a trailer Dad had purchased back to Channelview. Then I drove to our pastor's house and he welded side rails on it. We had begun packing and loaded the trailer and truck with all of our earthly possessions. October 31, 1982, we headed to the farm which would become home for Debra, the kids, and myself for a little while.

CHAPTER 6
Life on the Farm

We arrived at the farm and moved what we could into the house the rest went to the barn for storage. Mom and Dad were now in Mississippi on project, and he had been asking around to get me a job there. But it was the early stages and would be a while. Meanwhile, he left me several projects to accomplish on the farm. The largest was of course to start painting the house. The building phase had been completed. The metal siding had been stripped from the new section and T-111 had replaced it over the entire dwelling. Dad wanted that part painted so that was my first project. I also was required by the TEC to do job searches. I had to go to three places a week and file every two weeks. Well, I could only go to the same business in the two-week cycle so I had to find different places to go during each cycle.

We began painting the house with the yellow that had been picked out. A light but bright yellow. The project lasted about a week and on to the next chore. Cross fencing the place. Barb wire all along the perimeter and inside. Dad and I covered the outside along the road and then it was up to Debra and myself to fence the internal portion of the property.

Dad's good friend had purchased the old place to go along with his acreage, and he had Debra and me feeding his stock for him during the week. We would put hay out and ensure they were all cared for. We watched over his place, and he had odd jobs for me too. In the spring, it was time to sprig his pasture with grass. Coastal was the grass of choice. The grass would come in squares, we would separate into little sprigs, then walk behind the tractor with a trailer and sprinkle the grass into the pasture. Of course, he paid me to do that for him, and it helped buy groceries and gasoline. I still was having to file my TEC paperwork and we would have to drive thirty miles to Bryan, Texas, when I was required to come in person.

Well, after about two months of hitting all the places, I received a phone call. I had an interview with the local door factory about fifteen miles from the farm. I was going in as a maintenance helper. Changing hydraulic cylinders, saw blades, even building trash carts. But I worked every day with weekends off. Money wasn't spectacular, but it paid the few bills we had and put food on the table. We were attending the First Baptist Church now and had the kids in Sunday school.

The church had a revival, and I began to feel the Lord's calling me to surrender to preach. I talked with Debra about it again, and she had reservations. I allowed the feelings to subside and we continued with our lives on the farm.

We planted a garden. Corn, potatoes, and watermelon, we worked on the rows and of course cut the potatoes into quarters to plant in the ground. It was hunting season, deer season, and squirrel season. I didn't see any deer to kill, but I was able to kill a few squirrels for meals and we would catch catfish from the ponds and had fresh fish to eat. One Saturday morning, as I was in my hunting location, a large coyote came walking through. My dad's friend had ask me to kill one for a doctor friend of his to have mounted and this one would make a great mount, and they were also a threat to the livestock, I took him down with one shot. I made my way to him and poked him with the gun. He appeared to be dead with a pool of blood surrounding him, a clean heart shot, I tied a rope on his hind legs and began to drag him to the house. As I was dragging the carcass, I heard a loud almost growling sound, I spun around ready to shoot him again but realized it was just air exiting his lungs as I drug him over small humps in the ground. I drove down to our friend's place and placed him in his freezer for him to take to his doctor friend for mounting.

We were also spending time with the cross fencing and various other jobs around the place. Finishing out the cross fencing. Following the way Dad wanted it accomplished. I was driving in the pasture and the truck got stuck. I was able to pull it out with the tractor, but the transmission was damaged. Dad and Mom sent the money for the repair and I found a guy who could make the repairs to the transmission and he rebuilt it.

The job continued, and in March, my grandfather passed away. He was seventy-five and had lived with Parkinson's disease for several decades. My grandmother had refused to have him placed in a nursing home and had cared for him through it all. In the end, she was having to place his food into a food processors and the squeeze if from a bag into his mouth. That is what love truly is for better and for worse. We drove to Corrigan, Texas, for the funeral and burial. That went well, my uncle said a few words and shared the stories of his growing up. Mom and Dad had made it in from Mississippi, and we travelled together back to the farm. Our garden had just been planted and crops were coming in.

On one of Dad's travels back from Mississippi, it was time to bury the septic tank and get it working. Dad brought the tractor up, and using the post hole auger, he drilled three pilot holes. Then it was my turn to use a pick and shovel to dig. This was a labor-intensive project, my labor of course. Well, the hole was getting close and we stopped to measure the depth and circumference. A little more digging through that hard red clay and it was ready. We laid down a base of shingles and lowered the tank into the ground. Once in place, Dad began to fill it with water and then we covered the tank up after tying in the piping from the house and the field line into it.

Shortly after getting the septic tank placed, the crops began to bud and produce fruit. The corn crop was stunted and never grew nor developed into a mature plant. Our watermelons were just getting ripe when a deer busted them open with its hoof. But the potatoes crop and the red potatoes came in strong. We had a bumper crop of potatoes. We sold quite a few to local folks and that helped with our finances.

I wanted a dog and read an advertisement for a husky. We traveled to Bryan/College Station and brought one home. We named him Rusty. Our son was playing with him, and the dog scratched him over the eye and he required stitches. Debra had us get rid of the dog; she thought it had bitten him.

One evening as we sat in the living room, our son passed out behind one of the couches. We rushed him to the emergency room but they found nothing to indicate what had happened. Something was definitely wrong, but they said he must have just had a stomach virus.

Dad called shortly thereafter and said if I wanted a job in construction where he was, I would need to come there to get the job. I quit the door factory, and we packed up a few things and headed for Mississippi. Little did we know how God was guiding us!

CHAPTER 7
Life in Mississippi

We packed up a few things and had made plans to go to her mom and dad's for a visit before we left Texas for Mississippi. Well, those plans were blown away as Hurricane Alicia came through Texas on August 18, 1983. We travelled Highway 190 heading east and remained on that course through East Texas, Louisiana, and then a few more roads till finally we arrived in Mississippi.

Mom and Dad were living on a secluded piece of property in their 8 × 40 park type mobile home. We would all stay in it for a little while. Dad had become a deacon of Buck Creek Baptist Church. They had just hired a new pastor and were helping him move into the parsonage. We attended that first Sunday, and I wasn't impressed with him as a preacher that much.

Monday started the job hunt. I went to the personnel office on the jobsite and filled out an application. The man Dad had been speaking to about hiring me hadn't turned in a hire slip for me. Monday morning, I headed back home. Tuesday, the same thing occurred. Debra and I had discussed the length of time we would stay if the job didn't come through. We had given it a week and the week was beginning to wane.

Wednesday morning, still no hire slip, as I was sitting outside waiting for him to possibly send it through when the personnel officer came out and said he had a job opening for a few electrician's helper and the money was fairly good. I and one other person sitting by me accepted the job! I hired in that morning and was sent for a physical as well being given a tool list. I drove home and then to the larger town of Petal, which was close to where we living, and found a five and dime store tool store. I was able to purchase all the tools I needed. Thursday, I started the job and went through all the orientation. Then I was assigned to work in the tank farm area for a while.

That weekend on Sunday, we drove into Petal, Mississippi, and began our search for a church. I had purchased a copy of the local paper and found a church that sounded as if it fit our family. We found a church home there and began attending that church, eventually joining the church. I became involved in their visitation program and even became a leader of a group that the pastor was forming.

We enrolled our son in kindergarten, and he did a fair job. Life had settled down and our finances were getting better. I was working fifty hours a week and making good money. Learning how to bend conduit and pull wire through it. The company offered a training class after hours Electrical I, and I signed up to take the course. The craft superintendent was the instructor and he went into how to wire a house and many basics in how to install and design the wiring for a house as well as voltage, amperes, and the like. I was driving myself to the jobsite for those. The county sheriff and the state police occasionally had road blocks placed on the road to the job both north and southbound side. They were checking driver's license and license plates. I had purchased my Mississippi registration and had the inspection and tags from Mississippi, and I never was stopped, had they checked my driver's license I would have received a ticket, but since I had changes in the registration, they passed me through.

We had been in Mississippi about a month or so and were really crowded in that small trailer. Dad found a 12 × 60 used trailer and decided to purchase it. Debra and I decided to purchase the 8 × 40.

Our credit as it were would in most cases not allow us to qualify for a loan, but Dad had made a friend of one of the locals land owners. He went to his bank with us and told us to wait a few minutes. He went in and talked to the banker. When he came out, we went in, and the president of the bank made the loan to us. Papa Glenn had a lot of pull in that area. Dad purchased the other trailer and parked it behind ours. We were truly settled in.

My allergy problems had ceased and I was working every day. We would make church on Wednesday and Sunday nights. I would make visitation on Thursday night and Saturdays. I was working for God too but still had that lingering calling that I was resisting.

We met a couple, Ricky and Mary, who had been together a while too as they began to attend church. We would either go to their place or they come to ours and we would play cards or 42, the domino game. They were a very nice couple. We met other friends too. October came, and the church had a fall festival. Mom made costumes for all of us. Debra and I were Raggedy Anne and Andy. Our son was, I believe, a rabbit and our daughter a princess.

We went home for Thanksgiving at Debra's mom and dad's and spent time at the farm with a four-day weekend. We made it home late from the Houston area, but I was at work that next morning. Life was going well and the church was planning a revival meeting early in the next year.

We went home for Christmas that year. We rode in Dad's pickup with a camper shell. Debra spent much of the ride in the back and I changed with her for part of it. On December 21, 1983, in Houston, the temperature dropped below freezing, and then the next afternoon, it dropped again and remained there for five days, setting a record for longest period of below-freezing temperatures in the city. Houston's temperature fell below freezing for ten consecutive nights, bottoming out at 13 degrees on Christmas morning. When we arrived back in Mississippi, temperatures were in single digits. Even the toilet bowls were frozen solid. Dad's actually cracked in the trailer.

Debra was covered with a blanket and I traded off with her so that she could get warm in the cab of the truck. While riding with our children in the back, I led my son to the Lord; that was a blessed Christmas. When we arrived back the next week at church, he made it public, and a few weeks later, he was baptized. The revival at the church came and several souls were saved and others came forward to get their lives right with God. I too walked down front, but for a different reason, I surrendered my life to the ministry. Ricky and his wife had also surrendered to the ministry and we drove to Shreveport, Los Angeles, to look into a Bible college there. We viewed the campus and were offered scholarships to play football. I was now twenty-eight years old and not in playing shape. Ricky was a little older than I was. We both prayed about going to that school, and we both decided we just couldn't go to school at the time.

As time passed, we were finishing up the project, and I applied for a job at the facility we were building. God didn't allow me to get on with that company, but I was able to obtain a transfer to a project in Texas City, Texas, since I had worked eleven months straight with no days missed. We packed up what we could and headed to Debra's parent's home to stay until we could have the trailer transported to Pasadena, Texas. We had to find a mobile home park that would allow that size trailer, and I was working five to ten hour days again. After having been away from our home area and church for over two years, God was moving us back.

CHAPTER 8

Back Home for How Long

I was processed in on Monday and went to work. Debra's task was to find a trailer park for the trailer and then we would need to find someone to move it for us. I made a few calls when I arrived home, and we went and looked at the trailer park; we settled on one for the price we could afford and that would accept our trailer. We made arrangements for the trailer to be moved. Two weeks passed and the trailer arrived. We had to have an electrician come and okay the plug in for the electric company to turn on the power. All was taken care of and we moved into the trailer and had telephone installed.

Debra registered our son in school; he was a first grader now. As school began, his grades began to slip and Debra had several meetings with the teacher. She was told by the teacher that she wasn't doing enough teaching at home. She had been working hard with him to get his grades up. But he was struggling to make it. As the year progressed, he wanted to play peewee baseball and we found a league. His team was called the Raiders, and he began to enjoy sports. But the nagging issue was his grades just wouldn't go away.

Dad was starting to have the farm the way he liked it. We made a deal with them for the trailer. They had left Mississippi and he was now in Crossett, Arkansas. Coming off that project, we made a deal, traded the 8 × 40, which we had paid off, for the 12 × 65 and had it brought into the trailer park. We now had more room and were able to spread out a little more. We attended the church we were married in and rejoined it the first Sunday we arrived back home. I informed our pastor that I had surrendered to the ministry and was ready to go to work. A little while after arriving home and rejoining the church the need for a youth director came about. Debra and I became the youth directors and set out to minister to the teenagers. My pastor allowed me to preach a sermon, and I was licensed to preach the Gospel.

We begin to work with the youth and started up a Monday night Bible study in different people's homes. We also scheduled different outings and events for the youth. My job in Texas City had been completed, and I had moved to a job in LaPorte Texas, and then on to other companies.

As the school year ended, our son had failed the first grade and was to repeat. We knew something was wrong but just couldn't seem to get the schools help to pinpoint the problem. We were seeking answers and trying to understand what was happening. Debra's brother had struggled too, and he had eventually been placed in special education.

Mom made it a custom to have all of her grandchildren up to the farm for a few weeks in the summer. They have fond memories of those summers. There was a small curio shop called Fiber Magee's in Franklin, Texas, and the kids looked forward to going there and getting trinkets. They would also make their way to the ponds on the farm and our daughter was dared to go skinny dipping; she took the dare and Dad caught her and she was in trouble. Another incident they talk about was the time in which my youngest niece and my daughter got out of bed late one night and went to the refrigerator and ate all the cool whip that Mom had planned on using the next day. Then one night, they went and ate all the rice pudding. The four T's, as they were called, would get upset over being punished and decide to run away. They would always make it to the barn and their journey was ended. One evening, after they had been playing and gone to the woods, we received a phone call, our daughter had lost her glasses and we would need to go purchase a new pair of glasses.

Another incident as they were playing in the woods, our daughter stepped into a mud puddle and lost her shoe. They built a tepee of sorts and loved to play all over the farm; it was their second home.

Trips to the store could be exciting and embarrassing for Mom. One day, they arrived at the store and had been smelling a foul odor when they stopped; our son begin to investigate. He came out of the car holding a dead rat by the tail and saying, "Here's the problem, Maw-maw." Then on another trip as Mom was shopping, he comes up to her and in a loud voice confesses to her, saying, "Maw-maw, I farted." Of course, neither of these was all that amusing to Mom at the time, but they are now.

As our son began the year with a new teacher, his grades continued to slip. One day, Debra received a call and our son had a medical incident. The teacher described it, and when we went to the doctor and as we explained what had occurred, the doctor felt that he had a seizure. He referred us to a children's neurological clinic one of the best in Houston. They began a battery of testing and concluded our fears. He had epilepsy. They put him on medication. Debra received notes from the teacher about how he was conducting himself at school. While he would arrive home and go fast to sleep on the couch. One behavior at school, another at home, the doctors decided a change of medication was in store as the Christmas break came. Debra was weaning him off one medication and starting him on the other. That was a very trying Christmas for all of us.

With his grades as they were, the school decided to run some test. Turned out, he had what Debra's brother had, a reading comprehension deficiency. The school then recommended that he be placed in the resource program and we agreed. As he began to get one on one help from the resource teacher, his grades picked up a little.

In the meantime, as I was off work, I began to attend some Bible classes. Debra went to work where her mom was working. Mom and Dad were ready to stop traveling and he was preparing to retire. One night in 1985, we received a late-night phone call, Debra's dad was in the emergency room and had a heart attack. Her baby brother said Dad was stable and she didn't need to come; about an hour later, the phone rang again. Her baby brother was calling and saying that Dad's condition had grown worse and she needed to get there. Debra rushed the five or so miles to the hospital but arrived too late and her dad was gone at the young age of fifty-seven years old. The arrangement were made and our former pastor was asked to come and preach the funeral and her dad was buried in the Veterans' Memorial Cemetery in Houston, Texas. Mom and Dad came and supported Debra's family and Dad had completed his project in Paducah, Kentucky.

We had settled into our new church home, and I had become the fill-in for our pastor as needed. Our daughter entered kindergarten about that time. Her grades begin to slip just like her older brother's. When the school year ended, it was recommended that she go into pre-first grade. As the school year began, they tested her too and she too had the same learning disability as her uncle and brother. She too would enter the resource program.

One evening as we were sitting at home, the two of them became really quiet, and I went to investigate. Our daughter had long curly hair and our son and her decided to play barber; yep, you guessed it: he had taken a pair of scissors and cut a spot about one inch square to the scalp. I turned around and told Debra, "You might need to go in there," to which she did. The gasp she let out could be heard all over the house.

Around this time, a pastor called the school I was attending and needed someone to help him build a church and to lead music. I would be able to preach on occasion while helping him with visitation. The man that was in charge of the school recommended me and we began to travel to Manvel, Texas. I worked with the man on weekends and worked during the week at my regular job.

My job situation changed, and I was required to work Sundays for about a month and I was no longer able to help. The job completed and I had to find yet another job. Which was done fairly quickly and I was back to pipefitting. One day, as we were working to remove some pipe, three of us were suited up in full acid suits with breathing air. As we were cutting the line out with air saws, I had the middle level. As we begin to cut simultaneously, the fitter on top hit a pocket of product, the liquid came pouring down on myself and the fitter below me. We were rushed to the safety shower and begin to wash the product off. Then then moving the acid suit and finally the fresh air equipment. I was on my tools for about six months and then a layoff and another warehousing job.

Dad had retired and was on the farm by now. About a year passed and I was close to finishing the new job and was able to get on with my original company that I had started with, this time as a material tech in an office on the jobsite. This project was in Sweeny, Texas, area. I went to work for the first time on a computer with this position.

Dad, being retired, filed his income taxes and had a man whom he paid to file his taxes an error was made and Dad had to go back to work. He had to sell all of the livestock to pay the taxes and penalties. I was able to get my boss to hire him as a material tech, and we worked side by side for about a year.

Making really good money we made a decision to purchase a new home. This time, a 16 × 80 mobile home. Three bedrooms, two baths, a beautiful home. The dealer we purchased it from helped us to sell the 12 × 65 and we used the money as a down payment. The home arrived and we had it parked right in back of the old one. We moved from one to the other, carrying all our things. Dad showed up that morning, and to his utter dismay, we didn't have things in boxes. Debra and Mom begin packing boxes as Dad, myself, and friend moved the furniture. All went well and we were in the trailer. I went and purchased the A coil for the A/C unit and a friend of ours came and helped me mount it and he was licensed to charge the unit with Freon. A/C was working great.

Back to the church, we had been attending in Pasadena and now leading the music and directing the choir. Shortly after arriving back and starting to lead music, the pastor decided to resign. The man who came in as pastor had some doctrinal beliefs that we did not align on. We moved back to our church where we had been married. The pastor was suffering from cancer and eventually passed away. He left me his library, and it was quiet a large collections of books. Dad and I travelled together for a while until the company arranged for buses to transport employees from Pasadena, Texas, to Sweeny, Texas.

As the project begin to complete. I was able to secure a transfer and went to Port Arthur, Texas, on a job. Dad remained on the project to help finish it up. While I was working in Port Arthur and driving 160-mile round trip every day. Dad finished the project we worked on together. He had retired yet again and had filed for his Social Security. He had received his first SS check and was seeing his early retirement come to fruition. We had our daughter's birthday in September 1991, she was ten years old now, Mom and Dad had driven down to help her celebrate. The party was at the local skating rink and a good time was had by all. But that wouldn't last.

Dad had gone to the doctor for a physical on Friday before driving down and was waiting on results from all his blood work. Monday came and Debra received a phone call from Mom. Since my uncle that I had lived with was having cancer surgery, Debra thought that he may have passed away or had complications. But instead, it was Dad; he had passed away of a sudden heart attack. She couldn't call me with the news. She instead called the deacon of our church. I received a call from the deacon who was a longtime friend of the family. He informed me that Dad had passed away from a heart attack. I had to get someone to drive me to the parking lot, then drive home, pick up Debra and our children, all in the rain, and then to Bryan, Texas, to meet up with Mom, my sister, and her family. My nieces came to me for comfort the moment we arrived. We went to the farm that night and then down to Pasadena, Texas, to make the arrangements for Dad's funeral.

A few weeks after Dad passed away, I began to have health problems. One evening, I arrived home and Debra was not there. I knew she was most likely at the church her sister was attending. I drove there, and sure enough, she was right where I expected her to be. One look at me and she rushed me to the hospital. My blood pressure had sky-rocketed and my chest was hurting. But they found no problem with the heart at that point. They sent me to a gastroenterologist and he dilated my esophagus after running some test. But the pain continued, but I kept working and driving. I had been teaching a Wednesday night class, and the deacon decided to start showing a video series instead of my having to hurry to church, I didn't like it at the time but realize they were most likely thinking of my health.

During this time, the church hired a new pastor and we would eventually leave for a church that was pastored by an old family friend. We got involved and helped where we could. Our former pastor had taken a church in Cleveland, Texas, and the church was doing well. The church we had begun to attend was doing well also. The kids were involved in the youth group as our son was now a teenager and our daughter approaching her teen years.

Eventually, I would have a heart cath and CT scans performed and told the only thing they saw was that the bottom of my heart was not operating properly, but that shouldn't be causing the problem. Church members and some friends and family said it was stress from losing Dad.

A few years past and a job change for me occurred and things were going well. Our former pastor had resigned the church in Cleveland, Texas, and they had hired one pastor who left after about two months. I went up and preached a message for them and several wanted me as their pastor. But instead, another man was hired. The song director at our church had left and they were seeking a new song director. I was approached at that time and then things started to change for us. As things progressed at the church in Cleveland, I was ask to come lead music for them. We began to travel to Cleveland every Sunday. Then a church about twenty miles south of them was searching for a pastor and I was invited to come preach. Three Sundays in a row, I was there and things seemed to be going well. But we had made plans for a hunting trip to the farm, and Debra told the lady in charge that we wouldn't be there for that reason. They never called me back, while I was away though the church in Cleveland had lost their pastor. And I was offered the job as a bi-vocational pastor.

Mom had invited her oldest brother to come live with her at the farm. In a way to help her while helping him. Well, he is a strange type of man. He was always looking for a way to make a million while working as a salesman. Early in the 1960s, he had worked in a refinery and it had a fire. He had been burned badly of a great portion of his body and almost died. He would seldom come around for

Thanksgiving or New Year's when I was growing up. Now Mom had invited him to come stay with her. He had an invention he was sure would make him that million. He had presented it to a car company and tests had been run on it, but it didn't perform like it should, he accused the company of tampering with it. Then he began to mix chemicals for ant control. He had me video the results and they seemed to work great.

Mom had begun to travel to Arkansas; her sister, my aunt who I had lived there earlier, was now living there and Mom had met a man through her. My sister was expecting her fourth and final child and the C section was scheduled. I and the children went to the farm for a hunting trip and Debra went with her girlfriend to a craft show. As Todd and I were hunting and Mom with my sister, my uncle was out working and our daughter watching TV. Our son had been seizure free for several years and was no longer on his medication. As we were squirrel hunting, I heard him rustling the leaves and said shhh; as I turned, he was flat on the ground, having a gran mal seizure. I turned him on his side and called his name and he came out of the seizure. We went to the house, loaded up, and headed to the hospital in Houston. I told my uncle and we started the three-hour journey. Confirmed seizure, now he would need medicine again.

CHAPTER 9

First Pastorate

The first pastorate started out well enough at least for a first time pastor and family. We would travel up to church about fifty-eight miles one way on Friday nights and spent the weekend at the parsonage. While we would drive up on Wednesday nights for the service and come right back. By now, I had begun working for the company I am currently employed with. We spent the weekend visiting with the members as well as my studying late nights in the church's study. One evening as we travelled home, we witnessed a traffic accident. We stayed around as witnesses for the man who was in the lane next to us. Fortunately for him, we had stayed around because the young lady he had the accident with was trying to say he was at fault. Debra and I had to go to a law office and give a deposition as to what we saw occur. We never really knew how everything turned out, but we feel like we helped him win his case.

One weekend, we went up to help celebrate the fiftieth wedding anniversary of a couple in our church. When we arrived that Saturday morning, there was no water for the entire complex. As I investigated, I discovered that the water well motor had been stolen, the hasp broken to enter the pump house. The party went on with no water.

Shortly after becoming the pastor and wife, our twentieth wedding anniversary was coming. I made arrangements with a timeshare company to come and view their property in Florida. They would pay for our accommodations if we would tour their property. We decided to take a week and drive. The children would stay at the parsonage and the church members that lived across the street from the church would watch out for them. We made the trip with no problems. Toured the facility and received our free room. We went to Universal Studios and some of the dinner theaters and had a great time for our twentieth anniversary. Hard to believe that has already been over twenty years ago.

As things progressed, the church members begin to really want us to move to the parsonage. We decided to sell our mobile home and move to the churches. As Debra was talking to a lady in our trailer park, she mentioned that we were going to sell our mobile home and she stated that her mother-in-law had been looking for a place. The sale was conducted quite easily and we moved to Cleveland.

Our son now a junior in high school and our daughter in the seventh grade. They would make new friends as the school year began, and our son would become involved in drama and choir and then try out for the baseball team. The schools in Pasadena had removed him from the resource program because he had scored just a few points higher than required to qualify. He was struggling trying to make the grade because of the state laws he was not allowed to participate in any of the choir and drama performances. As the year ended and we attended the graduation, I talked with the superintendent of schools and he committed to having our son retested. He qualified for resource classes yet again for his senior year, which was great news.

Our son began his senior year in high school and was placed in resource classes. I was now commuting 160 miles round trip a day to work. We were settled in at church but having a hard time getting it to grow. I was teaching adult Sunday school, Sunday morning, evening, and on Wednesday nights. The deacon and I would go on visitation on Thursday nights and Saturdays. I would still have an occasional chest pain and feel like I had in the past. Even having some time in the hospital over it. Still no definitive answer to my health condition. We were serving the Lord though. Living in the country again.

Being in the country was great in many ways but had drawbacks. My commute to Houston was tiring, but I would work till 11:00 a.m. on Friday and get home so Debra and I could go out to lunch and spend the afternoon together. We would have some quality time together on those Fridays; they were an exceptional time.

Time neared and our son was graduating. The drama department put on the play *Little Shop of Horrors*, but he couldn't participate because of his grades. However, he was able to help with props and things. Graduation day arrived and his grandmothers made it down. One Friday night, he came to me and wanted me to drive him to the McDonald's in town to meet the marine recruiter. We had a discussion and I asked if he had told them about his epilepsy to which he said no, he hadn't. Saturday morning, we drove into town to McDonald's and before we got into a long drawn-out spill about the Marine Corps which by the way had been his dream. I ask the recruiter about our son's epilepsy and medication. To which he replied that our son could not go to the infirmary every day for his medication. He would not be accepted into the Marine Corps. I called up a local training school and had a recruiter come to the house to talk to him about taking AUTOCADD drafting courses. The recruiter went into a tirade about how I and my wife would kick our son out of the house if he didn't go find a job and upset him tremendously; he refused to even consider that school again. One Sunday after the morning service, the wife of the only deacon we had was talking with our son. Before he or I knew what was occurring, she grabbed him by the collar and proceeded to tell him just how he was going to look for a job and that she would take him around town if she had too.

He did find a job working at a local restaurant for a while. Then a friend's brother hired him as a yard helper for a pipe yard. Hot work but he was working. I would drop him off on my way to work and pick him on the way home. Until one day when we went to the local car dealership and he bought with Dad's help his first vehicle, a 1998 Ford Ranger. He eventually quit that job and went to work at a theater in Humble, Texas. That lasted for almost a year and then he was fired and an old family friend hired him as a store helper at a craft store.

Our daughter, now in high school, was also in choir and drama. She remained in resource classes and was listed in "Who's Who" of American High School Students. She had made friends and was working at a restaurant in town. Both were doing well and becoming adults.

Mom called me shortly thereafter and announced she was selling the farm and wanted to know if I wanted to purchase it and of course I did but I couldn't afford it. We made a few trips to gather things we wanted to keep. Mom gave us a table Debra had always wanted, and I went and towed the pickup Dad had purchased new, home with me. A 1982 GMC, it was in rough condition, and I ended up having to put a rebuilt engine in it. The farm was now gone. I happened to read an ad in the paper for a deer lease; it was just around the corner from the church and relatively inexpensive. Debra and I discussed it, and we paid the money for the lease.

We were able to access the property anytime and I set up a blind for hunting. Very few deer were killed, and the next year, the president of the lease attained a different property, this one had two fishing ponds on it. We would go there a few times and fish, and I set up a deer stand for hunting. We enjoyed our time on the lease and had some good time as a family.

As the weeks turned into years, Debra and I became the ones designated to show the lease in the offseason and sign people up for membership. I liked to go out on Friday evenings and Saturday mornings to hunt, and we would spend some Saturdays fishing.

Our son now having lost yet another job he and the lease president had become good buddies and he was hired to help with a remodeling business. He went all over the Houston area and the man would buy him lunch and pay him. One of his dreams was to become an actor, and I found an ad for an acting and modeling school. It was on the west side of Houston and my job was east side. We signed him up for classes and he would ride to work with me, then catch a city bus to the school. He graduated and received one or two jobs but then that fizzled out too. He found a job in construction as a laborer, and we had purchased a newer vehicle and wanted to trade the van in. He and I worked out a deal and he bought him a new car in which we traded in the van and I took over his truck notes.

As I enjoyed the lease, we had scheduled a revival and I had set time aside to go and distribute flyers for the service. My son and I went out that Saturday afternoon and distributed what we could. I planned on going to the lease and hunting, actually I went and sat in the deer Stand and would get close to God. Well, as I told the deacon's wife I was going hunting, she threw a fit, told me how the church and God were more important, and I needed to go out with more flyers again. Needless to say, I didn't go to the lease that afternoon.

I was getting laid off for a few months but had vacation time built up, so I was doing things around the church and house as well the lease. Debra and I were spending time together. The lady of the church came up with an idea to paint the church. She took all colors of paint she had and mixed it in a tote. We all began painting the exterior, and it came out a grayish purple color. We had finished most of the church, and I said I would finish the balance since it was late and we had church the next day.

The president of the lease brought his tractor over for me to work on. I was able to crank it and idled it up to a higher RPM hoping to charge the battery. I climbed up on the tractor engaged the clutch put it in gear and my foot slipped off of the clutch. The tractor lurched forward, and I flew off the back landing hard on the ground. Getting up my shoulder hurt me badly, I went into the house and my daughter cleaned up the cuts. Debra was at a game day for the ladies, so I drove myself to the emergency room and our daughter called her. Turned out I had separated my shoulder, fortunately I was already off work and then changed to sick leave instead of vacation time until my sick time ran out.

But the church still needed to be finished with the paint job. I was laid up in a sling and we received a call from our church lady across the street. She told Debra how I promised to finish painting the church, and Debra reminded her of my injury but she was insistent. There I was up on a ladder arm in a sling painting with my left hand. Trying to balance on a ladder. Finally we all finished the paint job.

My job called early in the next year and I was able to go back to work. This time on a project in a chemical plant. Debra called me one day and said guess where I've been, I said I didn't know she said at the church. The deacon's wife called and ask to meet her. She agreed and they went to church. The lady had brought a tape recorded with her and started it. The lady begin to list the things we had done right which were very few and then a litany of things that we were doing wrong. Debra and the children were dressed very nice for church, but my suits were old and not very nice looking. She wanted to know why Debra and the children dressed so nice, but we couldn't afford nice suits for me. A three-hour lecture ensued on the little good and litany of bad things.

I began to contemplate changing churches and sent resumes to several churches. One called me for an interview. And Debra I drove to the Oklahoma-Texas border to interview. Things seemed to go well except for one sticking point. We had dinner and went back to our room for the night. About midnight, we received a telephone call; our son was calling. He had gone to take a bath, and as he touched the shower curtain, a snake fell into the tub with him. Well, as it was described later, he jumped out, put a towel around himself, and ran into the hall. Then they called us and wanted me to come get the snake. We loaded up the truck and drove home. Upon arriving, there was the snake swimming around the tub a green garter snake. I grabbed it and threw out of the house. We never heard back from the church.

Another church called the church my parents had been married in and ask me to come preach on a Sunday night we weren't having Sunday night services so I agreed. I preached and then the church asked me questions to which I answered to the best of my ability. Well, there was one sticking point yet again. The church hired another pastor.

On my birthday in 2000, I was driving to work had to stop for gas in the truck. Then headed for my commute to the Houston area. As I was going around a curve, the back of the truck began to slide, and I turned the wheels into the slide just like drivers are trained to do. It righted for a split second and then I begin to spin the opposite direction turned the steering wheel back and then the front tire hit a soft spot. Now I was in full spin mode. Spinning several times until the right front bumper grazed a tree and the truck flipped. Landing on the cab in a ditch. I was hanging in the truck, found my cell phone, and called Debra. 5:30 a.m. I told her I needed her to come get me, to which she responded, "Where are you?"

I said, "I am down the highway."

She said, "How will I know where you are?"

To which I responded, "When you see a truck upside down in the ditch, that would be me!"

I could have heard a pin drop on the other end of that phone for a few seconds, then she said, "Let me get dressed and I'm on the way."

It was raining hard, but I released the seat belt and fell to the ceiling of the truck that was now the floor and rolled the window up which would open it now. I crawled out and was met by some people who had witnessed the entire incident. Debra arrived and we drove back to the house and I changed clothes; we headed back to the truck. DPS was now on the scene and investigating they ask if that was my truck and I answered to the affirmative. By now, the cab had filled with water and the electrical system was popping. A wrecker came and loaded the truck up, and he drove to the house where we unloaded everything and he hauled it off, and I said, "Happy birthday to me, no more payments."

My son was a little upset that his first vehicle was totaled, but he had a new car that he had just purchased.

Debra had been feeling badly, and after seeing the doctor, we were told it was her gall bladder and it must come out. I had asked the church to pray for my employment situation. My company had very little work, and I stated that I might get laid off again if things didn't get better so to please pray about it. I told my only deacon that we had a job coming in and I hoped that I would be assigned to perform the takeoffs on it. I didn't want to go to the job site because it was in Florida and I was the pastor and didn't need to go to that job in the field. Please pray, I asked him.

Christmas came and our daughter being in her last year of high school was preparing for graduation. Starting the final stages of school.

A school play and choir concerts for her, the prom too. My deacon had taken a church to pastor but didn't move his letter. As March came, so too did word on my employment situation. I was asked to work on the project in Florida but not as I had hoped it would be in the home office in Houston. The choice to stay employed with my company would be to go to the job site in Florida. Otherwise, I would be laid off and have to find a job. I began to search and ask the church to pray that I would find a job. Debra's gall bladder problem had worsened so the decision was made to remove it. We went to the out-patient center downtown for her surgery. Everything went well and we spent the night at her mother's house before travelling home the next morning. No major physical exertion, no lifting for six weeks.

Decision time had come for me on the job. What would I do and what decision would I make. I had been searching with other companies for a job. I wasn't being paid by the church at all; the little bit they had been paying at the start of my pastorate was stopped. The people decided outside of having a normal business meeting to stop paying me anything since we were living in the parsonage. The decision would need to be made and a short time to make it.

CHAPTER 10
Decision Time and Consequences

Debra and I discussed it, and since no other employment had been found, we decided it best for me to go to Florida with her and the children to follow after our daughter graduated. Two weeks before Easter, I would be leaving, and Easter that year was in April. I drafted my resignation for the church and announced that effective Easter Sunday, I would be resigning the church. That I had to leave in another week and then I would fly back for Easter and spend Easter with the church as my last Sunday.

The agreement with the church was that I received two weeks of vacation per year. Since this was March and a new year, my vacation time had begun. For about three years straight, I had not taken a vacation so it seemed reasonable to be able to take the time. Plus, they had stopped paying me any salary. I also asked what it would take in order for Debra and the kids to remain in the parsonage until our daughter graduated in May. We were at the end of March almost and had only two months left.

This was on a Wednesday night and the deacon who was now pastoring was not there. He called me up on Thursday night and ask me to meet him at church. When I arrived, he demanded my keys and said that I was no longer the pastor. I told him I had all books in the office and needed to get them out. He said he would unlock the office on Friday for me to get the books. Now the agreement with the church was if I resigned, I had two weeks to vacate the parsonage from the date of resignation which was still three weeks away. But if they fired me, I had a month to vacate. He said we had two weeks to vacate the trailer or we could pay a $500 deposit and $500 a month, which may be reasonable in today's economy but for a trailer with holes in the floor and weak spots, it seemed a little high. That and the fact that we were already in the place and wouldn't be leaving, it seemed like a deposit was a little bit of a stretch.

I said, "No, you just fired me. I have four weeks."

He said no, I had resigned and I hadn't built up my vacation time and had two weeks. He also said that I had lied and knew all along I was leaving and going to the jobsite. If you remember in chapter 9, I had told him I hoped I would get to work on this job doing the takeoffs. I meant in the home office and took it that I had said I was going. I reluctantly agreed to three weeks, and Debra and the kids would have to pack and we had to find a place to move. With just a few months left in her senior year, we really didn't want to move to Debra's mom's till school was out.

We made plans for a storage shed and begin to pack. I boxed up my books on Friday, and a man who had been attending the church volunteered to help us move and he disagreed with the way they had treated us. We loaded my books and other things on the trailer. The president of the lease had a house on that lease and told us we could move into that house and the only thing we needed to do was for Debra to show the lease to prospective hunters. We moved most of our goods into the house on the lease the next weekend.

But the transition week while I hadn't left for Florida and while working was a very hectic one. Debra having just had surgery two weeks prior could not lift any heavy things. She sat on the floor and loaded boxes as our son brought things to her. She loaded them the best she could, and we were getting things ready for that final move. We decided it would be best to get out in that first week. When I arrived at the trailer every evening, I helped with things as did our daughter when she arrived home from school. One day while at work, Debra called me; she was in tears. Three ladies, including the deacon's wife, were insisting that she had stolen the records for the church. Debra was the church secretary and had been keeping the notes for the business meetings. Well, they had insisted that those records were in the trailer and they wanted them almost forcing their way into the trailer. Debra asked where they were kept which I told her. They were in the sound room between the desk and a table. She hung up the phone and went to the church with them. Leading them right to the briefcase with the records. No "We're sorry for accusing you of being a thief," no "Sorry about trying to barge in," and nothing for calling her a liar. But they had their records and they were there the whole time.

That whole week seemed to go slow, and on Thursday, we were finishing up and preparing to move things to the lease. I took a vacation day that Friday, preparing to leave on Saturday. We were in the house on the lease that Friday night and had settled in. It was just amazing to us that people who had called us friends and one even had told Debra she was like a daughter to her had treated us as they had. Yet a man who very seldom graced the doors of a church would agree to allow us to live there rent free with the exception of showing the lease to perspective hunters.

The next day was one of the hardest days in my life. I had to leave my family behind and head to Florida. I was driving my son's car because of the gas mileage and headed out. As I pulled on the highway, tears were flowing from my eyes and I wept for several minutes as the miles apart begin to take me further and further away from my dear family.

I know it was just as hard on Debra too as our love for each other is strong, but it would be tested in the months and maybe years ahead. I headed east to Florida and made into the Florida panhandle before stopping for the night. Bonifay nearly ten hours from home. A five-hour drive ahead of me the next day. I checked in, went to get a bite to eat, and went back to the hotel and called Debra. Let her know I made it to the motel safely, and I would talk to her the next day. We had a lengthy conversation and finally said good night.

The next day, I awoke and headed for Lakeland, Florida. I called Debra and she was going to church in LaPorte to the church we had called home before I had been called to preach at the church in Cleveland. Then I filled the tank with gasoline and headed east to Tallahassee and then turning south toward Lakeland. Upon arriving, I checked into a motel chain that had monthly rates. It was near a shopping mall and had several retail stores in close proximity to it. It was also about five miles to the job site, making it a very convenient place to stay.

Again, I called Debra and she was spending the day at her mother's. We talked awhile and then she was going to take a nap as was I. When I awoke, I decided to try and find a church. There was one not far from the place I was staying and I went to their evening service. Then I went and purchased groceries for the week, and I arrived back at the motel. I called Debra back one last time before retiring for the night. The next day, I arrived at work, went through a short orientation, and then settled into the office I was assigned to and began my daily assignments.

During that week, I searched through the telephone directory and found the local SBC association. I contacted via email their Director of Missions and told him about me and asked about any open positions in the association or how I could serve God in the Lakeland area. Debra was still hurt by the treatment from our members of seven-plus years and was really hurting.

Well, upon contacting him, I found that he was serving as the interim pastor for a church and decided to go there on a Wednesday night. I arrived there, and they were serving dinner to everyone. I found and met Dr. Roberts and we had a lengthy conversation. He informed a few weeks later of a church in the association needing a song director, and since I had been song director at several churches, I decided to go and speak with the pastor.

It was decided that I would receive a try out to become their interim music director. That would also entail conducting the choir and having charge of all the functions of the music for the church. I led music that first Sunday and was called to be the interim by the church. The month went by fast and I flew home.

I settled into the job and the church and was feeling good about the decision to leave the church and come here to Florida. Plans were made to fly home for our daughter's graduation and then Debra would move to her mother's for a little while. The company said I would be paid for a trip a month, and I was receiving per diem on a weekly basis which paid for my expenses. One day while I was working, Debra called, very excited. She was sitting on the covered porch of the house on the lease and had seen a snake; she was very concerned. She said it was here then at the outdoor fire pit and crawling toward her. I tried to get her to calm some, but she was scared. As we were discussing what to do and what her plan of action was, our son drove up with my cousin and they never found that snake. From all indications and the description, it was a non-poisonous garter snake.

I would get out on Saturdays and take a drive to learn the area. For a Texan, Lakeland seemed a little odd. When someone would ask about where a person was living, they would ask if it was North Lakeland or South Lakeland. That seemed strange to me.

Debra and I had been discussing where I was living and discussing the possibility of purchasing a travel trailer to live in, many of the guys on the job were living in one. I looked at apartments as possibility too. But found nothing as nice as the motel for the price.

Debra flew in for our anniversary, and she stayed for a week or two. During that time, we looked at apartments and then settled on a travel trailer. Arraigned for financing and made the purchase. We then found an RV resort in which to park the trailer and found we could save quite a bit of money from my per diem this way.

She flew back home and her and kids moved to her mom's for a little while. The plan was for them to possibly come in August or September. But things changed, and well, I had to fly home for a quick trip.

CHAPTER 11

The Next Chapter in Our Adventure

Debra called one day and was crying and upset. Something had happened with her mom; she was ready to come to Florida. I made arrangements for a quick flight home one way, and we would drive to Florida. She picked me up at the airport, and we packed things in the pickup we had bought from Debra's brother and headed out late that evening.

Torrential rain was falling as we traveled through Baytown, and it ended just as we were crossing the Texas and Louisiana state line. We stopped in Orange, Texas, for snacks and sodas and begin the long arduous 962-mile journey to Florida. The wipers wouldn't turn off and kept screeching as we drove. I was trying to sleep in the front passenger's area. The children in the back seat while Debra drove the first leg of the journey. We changed drivers about the time we were crossing the Mississippi and Alabama border. We finally decided to stop and get some rest in the Panhandle Area of Florida.

Next morning, we had breakfast and then started the final portions of the trip. We arrived early that evening in the RV park and unloaded as the kids decided to venture out in the RV resort. They found all types of things to do even that they would be able to fish as the place had a lake on it. So a trip to the store for fishing equipment was at hand. Well, we made a quick trip to the store and stocked up on a few groceries and of course the fishing equipment. We all started life together in an RV. It reminded Debra and me of the old 8 × 40 we had lived in for those few years. The kids had ventured out and found some folks their age in the trailer park and were having fun when we arrived at the trailer with the groceries.

Next day, we went to church and they met even more folks their age. They would be able to get really involved with the young adults and the youth group. In retrospect, that was really what we all needed after the ordeal at the end of the ministry in Cleveland. Back to work for me the next day and things were going fairly well in Florida.

As the interim music director, I would wear very colorful ties and the pastor would try to outdo me with his tie. Very seldom was he able to do so. The family had joined the choir and we were serving here as a family. The church hired a regular music director, and I went to the choir. We were having an enjoyable time worshipping with everyone.

We decided to take the kids to a theme park in Orlando one weekend, and they had a great time. While we were over that way, we made a phone call and stopped by my cousin's house, they lived between Orlando and Lakeland, and we had a great visit with them. Then headed to the trailer. While in Florida, the church youth group had a trip to Georgia and our kids were able to travel with them on that trip. They were having a great time. Enjoying life for the first time in a long time. Our daughter loved Florida, but our son really wanted to be back in Texas.

On the project I was working a position for a janitor came open. I spoke up for my son and he was able to get the job. Two of us were working and the girls were by themselves during the day. We would arrive at the trailer about 6 and would grab the fishing poles and walk to the lake to fish. There was a pier and we would have the bait ready. Debra and our daughter would spend time at the office with the pool and pool table. Everyone was able to settle in and relax with life after the ordeal in Cleveland.

I was asked by a group of folks to coordinate an effort on Friday nights for us to have dinner at one of restaurants in the area. We went to the best steak house in Lakeland as well as seafood and Hispanic foods. The kids would go with us and we would be out as a family. The Northside Mall was not too far from the RV park and we would go there often. The theater was there and we'd take in movies.

Many of the same group we went out to eat with would venture into another means of entertainment with us. I arranged for us to have a bowling league. We would get together on a Tuesday, I believe it was, and bowl. My wife and I were on a team of three and our son was one another team of three and our daughter was teamed up with my boss and the procurement agent on the project. We pooled our funds and had everyone receive prize money at the end. Our daughter's team ended up winning because of her handicap and the guys she was bowling with averages.

Our daughter's birthday arrived, and she wanted to celebrate with her church friends. We had them come to the RV park and they played volleyball and other things, and we had hot dogs for them all. She had a great birthday and enjoyed her time there.

As time began to wind down on the job, it was getting to be time to leave. Debra and I didn't want to move back into Pasadena, Texas, area in the RV. We decided we could afford to purchase a house, and I began an internet search back home. I found one I felt we could afford and Debra called her best friend in the area to view it for us. She came back with ringing endorsements for us to purchase it. I made a bid and it was accepted. The paperwork was begun and loan approved. Debra and I flew home on the week of her birthday, took a walk through the house the morning of her birthday, and signed the papers.

We now had a home to go back too. We had decided to wait a few weeks with the bowling league to complete and other things happening in Florida, so we stayed a few extra weeks and I charged vacation time. I found a suit retailer in the mall and bought a few colorful suits, a purple and a blue. I picked them up on a Thursday before we were to leave and wore the purple an event at church, and that was it; the pastor said I won with that.

Our son was ready to get back home to Texas. Our daughter had made so many friends and had a boyfriend in Florida so she really didn't want to leave. But we were all heading back to Texas. As we were preparing to leave, we decided to have a transporter tow the trailer. Debra had arranged with her mom to allow us to park the trailer at her place for a while. I was doing a quick inspection of our truck and found that some bolts had sheared off for the plate in which all the accessories, alternator, air conditioner, all of them. A rush trip to a wrecking yard and a new plate was found as the other had cracked. Another trip to a store to purchase taps for a drill to try and extract the bolts which had sheared off in the block. A long hard day and we were able to get all but one bolts extracted. Finally getting the bolts in to install the used plate and all the accessories attached.

We rented a tow dolly to tow our son's car home. The trailer had already left and we were finally able to head for home. There were no problems on our trip home and one night in a hotel. We arrived at her mom's that next afternoon, the trailer had already arrived and was sitting in the yard next to her mother's driveway. The plans for the move into the house were made as we had to arrange for utilities and the like. So now our Florida adventure was over and a new phase of "Our Adventurous Journey" would begin.

CHAPTER 12

Going Home, What Next

We began the move into the house and things were put into place. Settled into the house as Thanksgiving came and went the time came for Christmas, the first time in this house we would be together. Christmas morning was a nice adventure as the kids were able to have some things they really wanted. We went to Debra's mom's for a family get together and then back home.

We were now back in our church we had joined, and they had a watch night service on New Year's Eve. They had their new song director in place, and Debra and I joined the choir. The kids were involved with the youth group and things seemingly had settled, but as things always seemed to settle, something else was brewing that Debra nor myself could have anticipated.

Arriving back home, work was very slow. They had a little work I could do, but it was looking as if I might get laid off yet again. But then a plant explosion occurred and the company I work for was contracted to perform the rebuild. I was sent to the job site and our son would be hired on later. He came in as a laborer but wasn't performing the way the superintendent wanted him too. My boss secured a transfer for him to work in the warehouse, and now he was working with me.

A note here: the same man who was now my boss on this job had been my dad's supervisor with the other company we worked for. He was now over both of us and had been the supervisor for three generations of our family.

About three months of work and then we weren't sure. As I came off this job, another project came about this project I would be sent to Texas City. This one was going to last about a year. The man I had worked for in Lakeland would be the material manager and he requested me as the material tech. He worked some things out that would help me be able to be assigned to the project earlier than my anticipated date in order to keep me employed, of course, God worked it out by human means.

Our son was able to participate in Special Olympics again, which made him happy. This time, our daughter was participating as well. The house was a 3 bedroom with 1 ½ baths and a single-car garage. We now had the old truck back as Debra's brother had been utilizing it while we were gone. Our son's Special Olympics coach helped secure him a job working as a porter at the local car dealership.

He has a great number of medals from his Special Olympics tournaments. Softball, basketball, tennis, and volleyball he participates in. They would travel over Texas to participate. He enjoys all the camaraderie with his friends and Debra's brother who plays also.

We decided it was time to sell the truck we had purchased from Debra's brother, and I purchased a newer one with our son's discount. He eventually began to have mini seizures with his epilepsy and was ask to leave the car dealership. We were taking over the payments on his car and decided to trade it for an SUV for Debra.

Our daughter went to work at a local fast-food chain restaurant just down the street from the house. She met up with a guy, and he had no respect for us or for her for that matter. He began to get her to spend her money on things for him. We begin to get notices from her bank that she was overdrawn. Then a grocery store chain called; she had used her debit card and overextended herself and they wanted their money.

We bailed her out for over $1,000 and she said later that we stole her money. She finally began to date another guy, but he was no better. She was spending everything she earned, and her bank finally closed her account because of the overdrafts. She finally left that boyfriend and started to talk with her ex-boyfriend from Cleveland.

Somewhere in all the mix of all her boyfriend saga, our daughter became pregnant. Debra and I believe she was drugged by one of her boyfriends and his friends, but of course, we are only conjecturing with that. It was about this time too that she met up with an old school mate from the Cleveland area. We befriended her and let her stay with us for a while. She too was a bad influence on our daughter and all things led to the pregnancy.

Two and a half years into the house and we are now going to be grandparents for the first time. We began to make plans for a nursery and our son would be asked to give up his room. The house had a large room off the garage that made a nice bedroom for him. We had to get a small window air conditioner and a portable heater, but he settled in and we set up the nursery.

As the time began to pass, the project was nearing completion and my company had to find a place for me yet again. Our department head was able to secure me a position with the purchasing department as an expediter, a job my dad had accomplished for many years. I was assigned to yet another office which was closer to home. For several months, I worked out of that office. As this assignment was nearing the end, our grandson was born, and as the assignment with expediting was coming to a close, I would be home only a few months but an assignment was close to starting. I helped take care of our grandson those early months. Our daughter had a new boyfriend, and he was wanting to marry her with the boy. His mother wanted them to move into a one-bedroom apartment, but we told them they would need a two with the baby. They ended up splitting up, and he went his way.

The time was getting near for my next assignment, and it too was going to mean I would need to leave town to work.

Before I was to leave, my wife's mother announced her and her husband were leaving for North Carolina to live. He had convinced her that it would be cheaper to live there than in Texas where they had a house which had no money owed on it. It would mean selling the house in Texas and leaving all her children behind. This entire time we had the trailer at her mom's and would now need to move it. We found a storage facility and decide to utilize the trailer.

Shortly after the birth of our grandson, she moved off and Debra's brother who has the learning disability and cellulitis would be left behind. At the time, he was living with a friend from Special Olympics and helping to care for him. Our son had found a place to work with the chain restaurant, unloading trucks and working in the kitchen. Again, he had a seizure, and Debra had to go pick him up. Yet he was and still is not able to get SSI or SSDI. His life has been a struggle. We keep praying things will work out for him.

We inspected several times a month and found that the floor was rotting out. Since it was under warranty, we towed it to a dealership for our brand and model, and they in turn had it delivered to the manufacturer's facility. Upon the trailer's return and with a newer truck, we decided to make a few trips. We towed the trailer to Purtis Creek State Park for a weekend trip, just Debra and I of course enjoyed the time away and did some fishing and went to a small church in the area. But we couldn't get the toilet to flush. I tried several things but nothing worked. Since the dealership was on the way home, we decided to drop it off to them. I received a call later in the week they had found the problem. It seems when the factory replaced the floor, they had forgotten to remove the tap that was over the drain and it wasn't able to flow. They had to receive permission from the factory to complete the repairs. We received the trailer back and then we towed it to South Llano River State Park, and here we could open the trailer door and enjoy seeing the deer graze. Just a good time being away together.

Financially, we were doing well, but we had some turmoil brewing in our home. God is on the throne and in control; we just had to trust Him to get us through all of it. Our grandson was a precious little blessing, and God was keeping a watch over him.

CHAPTER 13

Dad Away, Trouble Comes at Home

A new project led me back to Florida, this time the job site was in Bartow, not far from Lakeland. I made arrangements to park the trailer in the same trailer park we had been before. Hitched up the trailer and headed for Florida once again. This time, it would be for at least a year. Per diem would be great money and would pay for the trailer space and more.

I drove to Bonifay yet again and slept in a hotel room for the night. Leaving again for Lakeland area the next morning. The newer truck towed it perfectly and without incident. I arrived at the RV resort and was assigned the space. Backed the trailer in, hooked up all the utilities, and called Debra. Then I went to the store for groceries and other needs allowing the A/C to run and cool the trailer down.

Our grandson was now six months old and growing. Debra was going to fly in for a visit and brought him with her.

Hurricane Bonney was brewing, and we thought she might be delayed in coming; they thought it might hit the area, but instead, Bonnie went into Panama City, Florida. They were able to make it in. Upon her arrival, I went to the airport and we headed back to the trailer.

More weather news was on, seems like Bonnie was closely followed by Hurricane Charley who was gaining strength and would grow to 140 MPH winds. We went to church and Debra and the music director's wife found an instant friendship. They were in an apartment complex close to the RV resort. We were invited to come stay with them if Charley came in. The first night, Debra had me rent a cabin on the RV resort property, and we watched as the rain came down and the winds whisked by. Debra and I ended up in their apartment the next day as we had no electrical power even in the cabin so the storm passed, the flooding subsided, and we were able to get back to the trailer. Charley hit August 13, 2004.

Debra flew out a few weeks later; another storm was looming as she prepared to go. She was able to fly out and make it home. I, on the other hand, was in harm's way. Frances was heading for the Lakeland area once again a large and powerful storm was coming. Frances hit September 4, 2004, and Debra insisted that I leave the trailer, so I went to a hotel to weather the storm. The rain fell in torrents and the wind again was high; the hotel lost power, and the bottom floor was damaged. My room weathered the storm and I drove back to the trailer park.

Finally relief but then reports were Ivan was coming, yet another powerful storm. This time, my area of Florida was spared but not the Alabama-Florida border. Then came Hurricane Jeanne, yet another hurricane and landfall September 26, 2004, she landed almost exactly where Frances had landed and the trek came right through Central Florida. I stayed in the trailer for this one as she passed a little south, and we only had sustained winds of 50 mph; the trailer had withstood those before. Power had gone out yet again and then the water heater had gone out. I was able to have it repaired and power was restored in about two days.

I had joined two bowling leagues and was doing well; in fact, I bowled a 250 average 3 game set and the team I was bowling with was doing well. I was in choir and was given the part of Simon the Serene with a solo to sing. Debra was coming and she participated as well, dressing as one of the women in the crowd and singing with the choir. She had been sent the CD and a book to practice with. I flew home for Thanksgiving and Christmas, and we had a good time there. The pastor of the church and his wife had gone to a restaurant and he had a heart attack and died. They were seeking a pastor, and I submitted a resume and filled in for some of the services. Another man had begun to fill in for the Sunday morning and evening services while I had training union for the adults and Wednesday nights. They hired the other man as their pastor and I went back to the choir. A friend of mine from the job and another coworker met one night a week for Bible study in the first friend's motel room, when Debra came; she too participated.

A storm was brewing at the house that Debra and I never expected. Our daughter decided she was going to move out with her friend and her friend's husband. Debra called me crying and in a panic almost. Police had been called by a neighbor girl and the police told us we could do nothing to keep her from leaving with her son. Debra was distraught and our daughter left, grandson and all. I was not able to leave to come home immediately, and we discussed what to do. When you're nearly a thousand miles from home and something like this happens, it is hard to take, but God was with us.

Debra finally came to Florida with me for a few weeks, and she calmed down some. But she was still grieving over the entire situation and we were trying to understand the whole situation. Debra flew back home, our son and Debra's brother were now at the house, and she settled in. Our daughter would call periodically.

Time for me to come home came in June of 2005, and Debra flew over to ride with me. As we rode, I told her some of the stories about our vacations. As we crossed the I-10 Bridge over Pensacola Bay, I relayed the story of my mother's uncle who had been an Assembly of God preacher. He lived in Pensacola and had at one time owned a WWII patrol boat. He also had control of the horse my cousin who had been killed in a car accident had given his eldest son and that uncle had sold it. But the thing I relayed most about him was how they had come to Houston for a visit, and as they sat in his baby brother's home, the pastor Debra and I had been married by and attended church with for so many year had been invited to come visit with them. Well, my aunt who was married to this uncle was relaying how she had achieved a point of not committing sin anymore. Our pastor looked her straight in the eye and asked, "You mean to tell me you don't get on the phone and gossip."

Mom said her aunt never liked our pastor after that incident. As we came through Slidell, we talked of our trip to North Carolina when she was pregnant with our son and how sick she had gotten. As came upon the exit for Jackson, Mississippi, I relayed the story of the trip in 1971 or '72 when I rode with Mom, my grandmother, and my dad's brother's wife to a funeral in Mississippi for my grandmother's brother. How the car had problems and I was able to correct the problem and how we had stopped to eat a seafood restaurant and I had eaten the seafood platter. As we arrived at the storage facility, we parked the trailer and headed home.

I reported to the home office on Monday. Our daughter had moved from her friend's house and was now living with a man. She would call us almost every night to come pick up our grandson. She was either working or the baby was crying too loud for her man's preference. Some days, we would have just dropped him off with them, and she would call for us to come pick him up.

He was arrested and eventually sent to the penitentiary for robbery. Our daughter was pregnant again and wanted to come live at home with us. For the sake of the grandson, we allowed her to come back home. Debra wasn't too happy, but she allowed it. One night as I had gone to purchase something at the store, I arrived home to a panic, our oldest grandson had reached up and pulled a bowl of hot soup off the counter burning his ear, the side of his face and his arm. I wet a towel with cold water wrapped him in it, and we all entered the SUV and headed to the hospital. As we drove, I passed a police car, and our daughter yelled out the window at them that her son had been burned and they escorted to the hospital. The burns were severe and he was transported to the Shiner Burn Center in Galveston. We all followed the ambulance except our daughter who rode with her son.

Fortunately, no skin grafts were needed and they placed a bandage on the arm and his ear. When we were able to come home with him, we were instructed to change the bandage every night and doctor his arm with burn crème. However, the ear we were told to scrape the scab off it and then place burn crème on it. I had to hold him to keep him from moving while Debra scrapped it and then applied the crème. That went on for several weeks until he finally was healed enough that we were able to stop scrapping. He healed nicely, and today, you can't tell he had been burned.

Well, as I returned to work from Florida, I was assigned to perform takeoffs on a job close to home and eventually was sent to the job site. Our son called one day; the old truck had stopped running, and I came home, grabbed the tow chain, and met him. We towed the old truck home and Debra's brother, and we paid for a motor out off a wrecking yard. My son and his uncle put most of it together, but I completed the torqueing and bolt completion. Then we installed the motor and finished all the accessories.

We tried to crank the engine but to no avail. I checked all the connection and everything electrical, no problems found. Then I asked my son what steps he had performed in preparing to pull the motor from the truck. He had left the battery connected and stated something under the dashboard had smoked. I began to look, and there was a computer component type box connected to the ignition system. We located one in a used part lot and purchased it. We hit the switch, and it cranked. I then used the timing light and ensure the engine was in proper timing. It reminded me of how Dad and I had rebuilt the engine in my old green bomb.

Thanksgiving and Christmas arrived and things went fairly well as gifts were received by all. Two thousand and six rolled around and a new year. I was now working on the job site near the house and now going into the home office on Fridays and Saturdays to perform takeoffs for yet another project. We talked about maybe purchasing another home as our daughter and her son were in a bedroom together because Debra's eldest brother had taken her room. Our son was in the large room off the garage and a new baby was on the way. We decided we couldn't afford the new house at the time and remained where we were.

The trailer had begun to rot out at the floor and a persistent leak continued to plague. We were trying to get the manufacturer to replace the floor once again, but warranty had run out and they wouldn't continue it on the portion they had replaced. We weren't sure what to do. It was now paid for we no longer owed money on it, but it was really not usable.

The project close to the house was coming to a close as the new grandson arrived. News came yet again, I was to be assigned to another project, this one in Bartow, Florida, right next to the one we had constructed in 2004 and '05. This time, I was receiving a promotion and, with it, a company vehicle and gas card. The trailer in the shape it was and my not really wanting to live in a travel trailer we decided to rent an apartment.

Debra and I would fly to Florida and went apartment hunting. I found one fully furnished I would need my sheets, towels, and clothing as well as dishes, pots, and pans. We would still have quite a bit of the per diem money left over. I made my one-way flight reservation and bought a large suitcase, and off I went to Florida again. The man I had worked for on many of my out-of-town projects and one in the Houston area was resigning from the company and going to work for the client. I would take over his truck and his responsibilities.

He stayed about a day and a half and left me with the duties of a field material manager, overseeing all the material operations for a large construction effort on a power generating facility. The day, I arrived on the job, a fellow I had worked with on other jobs ask me who had performed the takeoff on the soil piping and I told him I had. He pointed to a very small pile of material and said that was all that was left, an almost perfect takeoff.

As material and pipe spools arrived, I could fell nothing but satisfaction in it arriving as I had performed all the material takeoffs for the piping material. The project went smooth with very few material problems due almost of the material being onsite from the start of construction.

I had joined yet another bowling league and was bowling several nights a week and on weekends. Something to do while alone and on the road away from family. With the apartment nearer the job than the RV resort had been, I had more time on my hands in the apartment. I had purchased a laptop to carry with me this time, and it quit working. I carried to the dealer I had purchased it from and had it repaired; it took a few weeks to get it back. I had purchased a game that was long and detailed to play and that helped with the time.

As the project begin to come to a close, another coworker was being assigned to a project in Tyler, Texas. We had talked about the trailer and all the problems and made a deal, he purchased it for half of what it was worth, but I was now clear of it.

He left a little before I did, but we stayed in touch. Once he and his brother begin to work to make repairs, the damage was found to be quite extensive. The floor that was supposedly replaced had been just the opposite. Seems the factory had overlaid one-eighth plywood over the rotted material and repaired it rather replaced it. The leak at the front of the trailer was not a clearance light leaking but a tear in the fabric of the roof and he had to replace wall studs and wood due to rotted material. I had been upfront with him about it and he made the repairs.

As the material portion of the project was ending, word came I was needed early for another project.

CHAPTER 14
Off to the Beauty of God

My boss secured an early release from the project in Florida, and I flew home, big suitcase and all. I was being assigned to a project in Billings, Montana, a beautiful city and state. I arrived home in the Houston area and was assigned to an office thirty miles from the house. We began preparations to go to the job site and worked on plans for the needs we would have. Debra and I had built up sky miles with an airline and decided to take a trip to Montana, which is where I was to be working, we went to find accommodations for me.

We flew into Boise, Idaho, yes, I know that is quite a distance from Billings, but the airline with our sky miles didn't fly to Billings. We rented a car and drove to Billings. A beautiful scenic drive. We crossed the continental divide and entered Wyoming back into Idaho and finally arrived in Billings. I had flown into Billings a few weeks before on a business-related trip. There was a restaurant that I wanted to take Debra too. Then we went apartment hunting, found a two-bedroom apartment fully furnished, all I needed was my clothes this time. They furnished everything for $1,500 a month, which included water and lights. The apartment had a washer and dryer right outside, a pool, and even an exercise area. We filled out all the paperwork and now had time for sightseeing.

Many of you may not realize it, but sixty-five miles Southeast of Billing lies the Crow Indian Reservation. You may ask what does that have to do with anything? Well, on that reservation, you will find the Custer Battlefield in pristine conditions. Very little has changed from the time of the battle, except for a national cemetery, a small museum, and of course the markers of where the men from both sides fell in battle and of course a five-mile stretch of road from last stand hill to the place where Major Reno and Captain Benteen dug in to await help. Then they have placards all the way to the Reno sight and back as to what happened at the different ravines and coulees. To me, Custer's battle plan can be seen clearly and the initial attack was the key to the plan and it was not fully carried out.

After some sightseeing and a few days getting to know the area, we drove back to Boise and flew home. What was supposed to have been a few weeks at home ended up being a few months. We enjoyed our time together as time to be separated yet again approached.

I was given the date of arrival and the company trucks were issued to those of us being assigned company vehicles. Since I had to have my clothes, and I planned on trying to go mull deer hunting while there I purchased a plastic storage container. Put it together and then placed it in the back of the truck with a lock on it. Debra was going to ride with me and then would fly back in a few weeks. We headed for Dallas-Fort Worth area as I begin one of my stories about going to Colorado for my uncle's graduation from the Air Force Academy and wedding in 1972.

As we drove and exited I-45 to connect to 287, we decided we would take the route Dad had taken to Palo Dura Canyon. As we were driving up 287, we came to a sign that said Esteline and the cutoff for Highway 86. I missed the turn, so we turned around and then turned onto 86. Now 86 will take you on a scenic route through Central Texas. But we went as far as Silverton, Texas. As we arrived in Silverton, we stopped for a drink and snacks. Then we turned onto 207 which leads to Claude. But before you get to Claude, you see two things on this scenic route. A Roadside Park on the brim of the canyon, when we arrived, the cactus were blooming and there was a large concrete pad the shape of Texas and the roadside park has an overview of Palo Duro. We stopped and enjoyed the view and photographed the beauty of the canyon before we continued to Claude. Right turn back onto 207 and down through the canyon crossing the little stream that is labeled Red River, it was very small with hardly any water in it. Then through the canyon and over to Claude and back on 287. If you've never driven that route, you have missed the beauty that God made for us. Then we travelled on to Clayton, New Mexico, and a place to rest. Clayton in and of itself has some historic places including the restaurant where we went to dinner. A good night's sleep and on to Raton Pass and Colorado.

As we travelled Raton Pass, we saw more of God's beauty, and as we travelled into Colorado, we made a stop for lunch. As we travelled, I wanted Debra to see Royal Gorge. We had been there in 1972 too. In 1972, we were able to park and walk across the suspension bridge, and they had a little train for the kids. As we arrived at the sight of the bridge, we found that they now charged admission and it might take longer than we had time for. We found a pathway to a fence and we could see to the bottom to the Arkansas River and the railroad tracks deep in the gorge. Back in the truck and trip to Pike's Peak. We travelled by the Air Force Academy and could see all the sights I saw on my trip. Debra says still today it was a great adventure to see the stories I told of growing up and vacations come alive in our trip.

As we arrived at Pike's Peak, we had enough time to drive to the top, so we paid our fee for the trip up the mountain. It was great as we started up, but the higher we travelled, the more Debra became very apprehensive. As I would point to a beautiful view or something down the side of the mountain, she would say keep your eyes on the road that is steep over there. As we arrived at the point where the asphalt ended and the dirt began, Debra grew even more apprehensive. As we travelled up the mountain, getting into thinner and thinner portions of the atmosphere, the truck showed signs of overheating. At the 12,000 foot mark, there is a place to park and raise the hood for the engine to cool down. When we arrived at this halfway point and stopped to let the engine cool, it was raining and the road was closed that led to the top, so we were required to turn around and head back to the bottom. Now the dirt road was a muddy road and the truck was slipping and sliding, which again made Debra apprehensive. Once to the lower levels and out of the park, she jokingly said, "Let me out to kiss the ground."

We made our way back to the interstate and drove north into Denver where we passed the Bronco's stadium and continued on for a few more miles till we stopped for the night at a hotel. The next day, we continued the trek north into Wyoming and then into Montana. We finally arrived at the apartment and settled in after unloading a quick trip to the grocery store for supplies and then back to the apartment. The project manager for my project had rented the apartment next to me, and when Debra would come to town, we'd go to lunch together. She stayed two weeks and then home. My friend and I had the Bible study with in Florida was assigned to this project too, and he ask me where we were going to church out. I had found a church down the street from my apartment, and we settled in at that church.

I began to investigate the hunting rules and places to hunt. In Montana, there are BMA properties and you purchase a license and the number of tags you want, antlerless tags were less expensive than the tags for an antlered mule deer, so I purchased a tag for the antlerless. Then went to the local wildlife office and found maps of the BMA area up in Roundup. That was about an hour-long trip.

I also talked with the pastor, and he provided the contact information for the local SBC association in the Billings area. We set up a lunch date and sat and talked for a while about churches. Other than one speaking engagement, there was not much I was able to accomplish in ministry there in Billings.

As hunting season came, my friend and I made a few trips north to Roundup, on one hunt we spotted deer moving across the plains and begin to track them. As we came to the top of a hill and were blocked in the cedar trees, we stopped to catch our wind. My friend pointed behind me and there stood a beautiful mule deer with the biggest rack either of us had seen. Neither of us had a buck tag, we watched him walk off into the foliage. Another walked up a little bigger than the last one and the rack was even bigger as he walked into the brush. Yet the biggest one ever came out from behind them and walked right past us.

Then we moved on to try and spot the herd we had seen they had already moved into the valley and were long gone. We made several trips, and both finally downed the meat we were hunting, I sent mine home in a freeze-dried package after having it processed.

Thanksgiving approached, and I booked my flight for home and back. As the day before Thanksgiving arrived, I had booked the last flight out on a specific airline. We boarded the plane and had settled into our seats. The plane disembarked from the gate, and we finally made it to the runway. As the engine begin to roar and the plane taxiing up the runway, the engines were throttled down and we returned to the gate, there was a problem. They deiced the plane more, and off we went to the runway. Again, we started down the runway again, they throttle down. This time, we disembarked and they found me a flight on another airline. I made that flight into Denver, but my connecting flight to Houston had already departed and the only thing they could do was find me a flight to LAX and then to Houston on yet another airline. Off to that other airline and off to LAX. We arrived in LAX and around 11:00 p.m. I was to have arrived hour many hours before and was still thousands of miles away. As several of us from our flight approached the counter for boarding passes, we were told the flight to Houston was overbooked, and they might not be able to find us a seat. Finally 1:00 a.m. Los Angeles time, we were seated and embarked from the gate. Finally arriving home around 8:00 a.m. Thanksgiving morning, a normal six-hour flight had turned into an eighteen-hour flight.

Thanksgiving and the weekend over it was time to fly back to Billings. This time, I boarded the plane and we were pushed away from the gate and then sat on the tarmac for another hour or more. The printer in the cockpit wasn't working, and they were waiting on terminal crew to print out their flight plan paperwork. Finally in line for departure. Up arrival in Denver, I arrived at the gate and you guessed it my flight to Billings had already departed. There were no flights to Billings until the next morning. I called my friend to see about him driving down to pick me up, but after a conversation, I decided to let them put me up for the night and fly in the next morning.

Then a Christmas arrived and I flew home, no problems this flight and Debra was flying back to welcome the New Year in with me. We flew back and I told her to wait till I got the truck. I pulled up in front of the terminal and loaded everything in the truck; she stepped out into the wind and said, "You need to get me a flight home, it is cold here," but she got in the truck and the seat heater kicked in. We arrived at the apartment, and when we were out of the wind, she said it really isn't that cold. The temp was around 10°F.

She hoping to see snow while on this trip and she got her wish, about twenty-five inches hit. She went out and enjoyed the snow, and we had a great time bringing in the New Year.

Next she flew in for our anniversary in June. She arrived and we made plans for a weekend trip. We drove to South Dakota and Saturday morning, we arose and went to Mount Rushmore. Took the entire tour with a guide and all learned the history of the sculpting of the presidents and why each one was chosen. We drove back to Billings, and since I had Monday off for a client floating holiday, we decided to take in Yellowstone Park. I called for reservations and booked a cabin at Roosevelt Lodge. I asked the booking agent the best route in to Yellowstone.

He told me to come through Laurel into Red Lodge and through Bear Tooth Pass. This would bring us in through the north entrance. Keep in mind, this is June, and we are driving as instructed. As we begin our ascent into Roosevelt Lodge, we begin to see snow on the ground. Reports were they had had about thirty-six inches on the tops of the mountains. As we ascended and I began to point things out below, Debra again says, "Keep your hands on the wheel and eyes on the road, it's a long way down."

We stop at one point for pictures and then continue our ascent, reaching the peak and the snowbank was a good 1 ½ foot above the cab of the truck. Thick white beautiful snow in June no less. The cabin had virtually one room and a potbelly stove. The restrooms and showers were in the center of the complex a few hundred feet away, I placed the packets for the fire in the stove later that night after dinner at Roosevelt Lodge and a walk on the paths next to the stream. We used all the fire packets that night to keep Debra warm; it had gotten into the thirties in that cabin.

With the two grandsons along with our children and Debra's brother, we decided to purchase a new home. It was being built and we would close in August. We made plans for me to come home and help with the move as we closed and began our move. We had hoped the old house would sell but to no avail. We needed the room and the space so we made the move. Debra's brother decided to stay at the old house while all the others moved in the new house. Five bedrooms, three baths, over 2,000 square feet.

We had moved in, so time for me to fly back, and Debra was flying back to spend a few weeks with me. While she was there, news reports came that a hurricane was forming in the Gulf of Mexico. Ike became a hurricane and was threatening the Houston area. We decided to get everyone on a plane again. Debra's brother decided to ride it out. Our two children and the two grandchildren flew up. They were on the last flight out of Houston. Ike made landfall September 13, 2008.

I rented a minivan to hold everyone and they arrived safely in Billings. On the weekend, we drove to the Custer Battlefield, then we went to Yellowstone and Old Faithful. They toured the city and other things on this trip a vacation of sorts. Our oldest grandson, now four, was excited over all the animals and things in Yellowstone as well as the herd of antelope that made their home in our apartment complex. Finally, word came they could head for home and all boarded the plane and arrived safely home and found only minor damage to our home.

The end of September came and as it was planned for me to be in Montana until the end of the year, things quickly changed. My boss in Houston needed me for another job and he requested my release from the project. Off I was, going to yet another assignment. This time, I would not have a company vehicle. A quick search of the internet and I found me a truck, huge discounts on it due to hurricane damage, which you really couldn't see. Debra went and looked it over for me and I called the bank to get the money. Then booked her flight to Billings and she would ride home with me. We loaded up the cabinet that I had bought for the truck and we headed home.

CHAPTER 15

Another New Adventure

I left the beauty God created that is called Montana. We drove home. I went to the auto dealership and we purchased my 2008 truck and I turned in the company vehicle. We drove to Baton Rouge and rented an apartment. It was furnished and a high rise building. The floors were painted concrete and it was about ten miles from the project I would be working on. But you could the stadium in which LSU plays and on game day you could hear the crowd noise. Venturing out on those days was sometime difficult as the apartment building was located on the same street as thee stadium.

The man I had replaced in Florida had returned to our company and was retiring. I was replacing him yet again. The day I arrived, my longtime friend who was over the warehouse managers and personnel came to the job site. As the man I was replacing left, so too was my friend there to fire the warehouse manager and a new one was assigned a man I had worked with a few years back while in Florida. So changes at the top of the material group came on that project at the same time.

I drove home as frequently as Debra and I agreed was financially possible. Still receiving per diem so the apartment was covered again.

But we now had my truck payment, Debra now had different SUV. The truck was getting broken in, and mileage was already building.

Debra came back with me for her birthday, and we went out to a seafood restaurant and enjoyed our time together. She stayed a few weeks and then we drove her home. I could never really settle into a church here, and the frequent trips home made it where I was attending our home church a little more often. Five hours away was not really that far.

As this project came to an end, another was looming for me. This would reunite me with a varying group of people I worked with before. The man from Montana who was the project manager was to be the construction manager. The field purchasing agent was on the last project in Florida. The friend from Florida and Montana that I had Bible studies with would be on this project. Then I hired two people for warehousemen that had worked with me or for me on other projects.

Three months in the home office making preparations for the project. This time, it was in Texas but still five hours from home, Tyler, Texas. Debra and I made a trip up to find an apartment. We found a real nice one, almost a brand-new complex on the west side of town that was secluded. Not far from stores and restaurants. We bought some furniture and set it up brought an old couch now I was in the apartment.

Our daughter had married a man who had been our son's best friend in elementary and high school until the move to Cleveland. He had been in prison and had been an overall messed-up guy. She hoped to keep him straight and we allowed them to live in our home. I had bought me another pickup and they were utilizing Debra's SUV, and he was going to make the payments on it to us. Debra was driving my 2008 I had purchased when I came back from Montana. He was supposedly working but never brought home a paycheck.

Again, I would drive home as many weekends as we felt necessary. One such weekend, we attended a shower for my nephew and his fiancée. Our son-in-law stayed home and said he had to work. Debra was going to come up to Tyler with me while the rest of the family was heading back home. When they arrived home, the house appeared to have been broken into. Televisions and a few other items were missing.

No apparent damage to any doors or windows, a strange break-in. We had an alarm system installed and still have it today.

A few weeks later, we received a call the alarm going off yet again and our son-in-law had been home alone, we had accidently set the alarm for away. Well, he didn't know the code and couldn't shut the alarm off. He ended up on the ground in hand cuffs until Debra arrived and had him released. Nothing was missing, and it was ruled an accidental alarm.

Debra would come spend time in Tyler with me, and we went to an upscale restaurant for her birthday in downtown Tyler. Our oldest grandson made one trip up and spent about week with us. It snowed in Tyler that winter and I sent pictures home. I had found a church that I attended while in Tyler, and while I disagreed with some of his beliefs, I found nothing better.

This job was a shorter duration, and soon, I was coming home with no project to coming up. A layoff appeared to be coming yet again.

This time while home, I decided it was time to further my education. I was still employed and working on various projects. I did some research and found Louisiana Baptist would do correspondence-type courses. I was a few classroom hours away from having a bachelor's degree so I enrolled. I was sent a syllabus for each class I was taking and purchased the textbooks required. I began to study, and as I read through the textbooks and answered the questions in the syllabus, I would come to various stopping points. At these points, I would either take a test or write a paper. If I was taking a test, I would take it to church and take it in front of someone who would sign a form, stating I didn't use my notes. I completed my courses just as the New Year began and would receive my degree in May.

Just as I completed my course, I also was laid off from my company. But a man I had worked for way back in the late 1980s and who had worked for my company for a while needed a warehouse manager to go on a project and I was hired to go.

By now, our son-in-law had virtually abandoned our daughter who was now pregnant. We couldn't locate him and he had our SUV. Calls to the police were of no avail. I was working for the time being on the west side of Houston awaiting the time to head for the new project. February came and the birth of our granddaughter the week before I was to leave for the new assignment and still not son-in-law.

I headed to Fort Stockton, Texas, a good nine-hour drive from the house and still about four to five hours to El Paso. Texas is a big state to cross. The first week or so I stayed in a hotel while searching for an apartment. Finally I found a two-bedroom on the north side of town. Not far from a Baptist church just a few blocks away. I would need furniture, so I went home and brought the bed and dresser but needed a couch and dining table as well as a television. I went to a rent-to-own store and found a couch and high back chairs. All would be delivered. I bought a TV stand and a folding chair in the meantime. I had a phone setup and was now again on my own with Debra taking care of the affairs back home.

Debra rode back with me on my next trip, and we went to the local restaurants and did some sightseeing. She wanted a few things for the kitchen and décor, so we bought those items and the apartment now had her finishing touches.

I was able to secure a week off in May for graduation ceremonies to receive my BA in biblical studies. We went to Shreveport, yes, this was the same school I had visited years before and didn't attend; it had a name change but still had its roots to back in that time. We attended workshops which were mandatory for me and had a great time. The night before graduation, we attended a banquet for the graduates, which had a nice dinner and speakers. The next day was graduation and my niece drove Mom down from Arkansas to attend. She finally saw me receive my college degree.

Then I headed back to Fort Stockton. Our anniversary was coming up so Debra flew into Midland-Odessa airport. We went places on this trip being in Fort Stockton that I had visited on the trip in 1972 when my uncle graduated from the Air Force Academy. I had talked about that trip many times to Debra, and now like the Montana trip, she would see those memories come to life for her as we continued Our Adventurous Journey!

The first trip, we went to Carlsbad Caverns a trip not far from Fort Stockton. We too entered through the cave entrance and begin the long arduous journey down the trail. Neither of us sure we could physically make the trip but willing to try. We went deeper and deeper. Then we came to the point that was halfway and were ask by the hostess if we were all right to make it. We said yes and continued the trek downward. Debra's back and knee were beginning to hurt her, but she wanted to make the entire walk and we were committed. They have benches at certain points so we would stop and rest. We arrived at the point of no natural light and continued down seeing the beauty that God made. Finally arriving at the café area and time to head to the top. We boarded the elevator with others, and within a minute or two, we were at the top. A trip that had taken several hours walking down lasted a very short time on the elevator. As we were driving back to Fort Stockton, we talked about the two trips I had previously made to the Caverns. How we went when I was about four or five and only parts of the caverns were opened and the bats flew out as we entered and then the trip in 1972 when more had been opened, and I had started feeling bad on that trip. How we left the Caverns in 1972 and stopped in Pecos to see the replica of Judge Roy Bean's courthouse. On our way back this day, we stopped and took a picture of that replica.

The next weekend, we made plans to go to the other place we visited on the 1972 trip Balmorhea State Park. This again is another beautiful place in the hot desert area of West Texas. The park has a motel for overnight accommodations as well as staying for a week or two. It a large swimming pool that is fed from the San Solomon Springs and the water stays 72 to 76°F year round. I told her we had camped in our tent and gone swimming in the pool. As you get into the wading area, the fish swim with you. How in the deepest portion it is about twenty-five feet deep and people scuba dive in it. Many saying there are catfish in that area as big as they were. They have a high dive and low dive for diving enthusiast and they are on the opposite site of the pool from the wading area. We paid our entry fee, then she and I went and changed to our swimsuits. The water was as they said cool and clear, just as I remembered it. We spent a few hours at the park in Toyaville, Texas, and headed back to Fort Stockton. Again, she said she saw my stories come alive as we lived them together.

I went home in August, and Debra was coming back with me yet again. This time, we decided to bring our oldest grandson with us. The next weekend, we took him to Balmorhea and he enjoyed himself. We also utilized the apartment pool, and I drove down to the job site where he saw the javelinas and deer. Fort Stockton also has a statue of a roadrunner and some other historic sites and placards. We took him to all of those. As we drove to Fort Stockton and his six-year-old mind was viewing the beauty, he'd point this plateau and that one looked like a volcano and he loved all the beauty that God created.

Debra and I discussed something that I had begun to think about and would follow through with when she had come in June. The pastor at the church I was attending in Fort Stockton was receiving a degree from a school through correspondence. I had communicated with LBU about going on and working toward my master's degree. Well, the school that the pastor was taking courses from was well pleased with them and I began to check them out. All courses required listening to lectures and taking notes from those lectures. Periodically stopping the lectures in order to take test along the way. Studying the notes prior to taking the test and then mailing the test back to the school for grading. Then continuing on with the lectures. I enrolled and began to study once I had all my CDs. I would spend two to three hours in the evening and weekends listening and taking notes. I would also rerun the CDs on my drives home trying to hear something I could retain as I drove. I began in June working on these taps and completed all courses by December, you can work at your pace, but I had completed them with the dedication I had to accomplish this.

Since I had paid off my tuition and completed my courses, Debra and I discussed going on to get my doctorate. More CDs and time, but I had time all by myself so I ordered my course CDs and begin listening to yet more lectures on CDs. Now let me note here there are many who feel that this type of degree wasn't earned but is a diploma mill-issued degree. To them, I say you try it, you take the hours of sitting and listening to lectures on CDs and you study your notes to take your test, then you tell me that it wasn't worked for or earned. I completed my studies for my doctorate, but not before I had come home and so I took them at home. I would then receive my doctorate in June at the graduation ceremonies in June.

Before the end on my tenure in Fort Stockton, I received a phone call from Debra. She had received a check in the mail from an insurance company on our accident claim. Well, neither one of us had had an accident, and it wasn't from our insurer. I made a phone call and this company was sending a check to pay for repairs on our SUV, the one our son-in-law had possession of and I was told he had taken to their adjuster and said he had our permission to have repairs completed.

I told her he had no permission and did she know where the vehicle was located because we hadn't seen it in six months. That set her aback some, I also informed her that not only was it missing, but I wanted that check cancelled out, and once the vehicle was found, then we would instruct her how to pay for the repair. My insurance company had called too, they wanted to know about the accident with my vehicle and how the folks driving it had sustained their injuries. To which I told her the story and didn't know the folks driving or the passengers, they still paid off because my permission to my son-in-law carries over to whomever he gives permission to drive it. I contacted the police to see what could be done about finding the vehicle. I was told since I had given him permission to drive it then it wasn't considered stolen. My only option was to send a registered letter to my home since that was his last known address, stating he no longer had my permission to drive that vehicle, and when it was returned, I could then call it stolen. I sent the letter and then the search was begun. They found the vehicle in a bad part of Houston, almost in the downtown area. It was towed to an impound yard, and my son went with a wrecker driver friend and had it towed to the house. Then we had it taken to a repair facility and the check sent to them which Debra had to sign once repairs were completed.

Then time came for me to come home, a layoff, but again, I was rehired by my company and returned to work for them. But with a twist, I would be in the offices around Houston instead going out of town.

CHAPTER 16

Coming Home to Win Her Heart

I completed the month of January with the company that had sent me to Fort Stockton. Then was rehired by my current employer whom I have overall nearly twenty-five years with. This time, I would have yet another position change this time I would be assigned as the project material manager on projects. 2012 is beginning with me home. Having been on the road for over ten years caused a strain on our marriage and our lives. Yes, we spent a few weeks at a time a few months at a time together. But Debra had been home and through many things with me gone.

We still love each other that will never change, but she is accustomed to being alone to do things with our son helping in some cases. Long-distance relationships can strain and even break a marriage, the love and commitment must be strong for it to last. Ours had lasted, but I would need to try and understand what was happening.

Since her SUV was now paid off and running, we weren't sure of it and what had been done to it we decided to purchase a newer one. We traded the 2007 pickup I had purchased and we bought her a 2007 SUV less miles and in better shape we thought. Our daughter had now begun to date since her husband had left and her boyfriend wanted the old SUV. Debra struck a deal with him for it, and he agreed to make payments.

Then the husband turned up and wanted to start seeing his daughter. Debra and I didn't really like the idea, but there wasn't much we could do about it. He would keep her on weekends. Again, he was supposedly working somewhere but no money. We ask our daughter about a divorce, and she contemplated getting one. Then just like that, he had disappeared before he was gone again.

Our daughter went to see a lawyer, but unless he could be served with divorce papers, she wouldn't be able to get a divorce. Again, the search was on. She eventually heard from a friend of his he was now in California. Living on the streets and no job. But unless he could be served, no divorce.

At the same time, our daughter and her boyfriend had broken up, and he now owed Debra for the vehicle. She received only about two payments from him, and he had lost his job. Then we heard he found a job and had a new girlfriend. Well shortly after that, we received a call the SUV he was buying from us had been stolen from his job. Then a letter from an impound yard: the SUV was found, but only the chassis and frame were left, we left it to the impound yard.

May came and graduation for my doctorate. I had still spent my time studying and testing. We drove to Slidell for graduation. I had found in my family tree searching that my mother's great-grandmother family had lived in Slidell, she had been orphaned as a young girl and her father was quite prominent in Slidell. In fact, Gause Boulevard is named for him. It seems he had a plantation on the Pearl River and would cut down and haul logs into the town where he had built a saw mill and Gause Boulevard was the road that was established in those days to transport those logs. We went to see if we could find his and for that matter my great-grandmother's grave they are somewhere close to the end of Gause Boulevard on the East End. But to no avail. We drove over to Perlington, Mississippi, and found quite a few of my ancestors' graves.

Graduation went off great, and I now had completed my doctorate. They had meals for all of us and then we began our trip back home. As we travelled, we talked about all the pictures we had taken of the headstones and how I wished that my maternal grandmother was still alive so I could finally settle for her who her grandmother's parents were. She had ask me to find out and finally I had.

Our daughter was still trying to locate her husband in order to be able to get a divorce. Then more word from his friend in the area, he was now living as female in California and had an apartment. She was working with her lawyer to get him served. It took a few months and nearly a year, but finally, she was able to get him served and have the divorce finalized.

With me now fairly steady in the offices around Houston, I began a search for a church to pastor. I looked for bi-vocational as my job would provide for our finances. I sent out several resumes including one to a church in Arkansas if God wanted me to leave and go out of our area. Well, that church some interest and then they decided to hire someone else. More resumes and finally a call came from a church forty miles from home.

Now April 2013, I received a call to come preach for them. Everything went well, and they wanted to hire me as their pastor. I requested a three-month interim in order for us to get to know each other and see how it was going to fit. In August 2013, I was voted in as the pastor. We purchased a travel trailer and parked it behind the church.

Things were running fairly smoothly that year. Debra and I made trips for our anniversary and we made trip to my mom's to get my grandmother's piano in October. I failed to ask Debra if she wanted it at the house. She had always wanted a piano, but I failed to ask, I was accustomed to doing things sometimes on my own since those years on the road and she was accustomed to doing things on her own we still have to correct that or at least I do.

We had a watch night service at the church that year to bring in 2014. We were staying in the trailer on some weekends and had done some visiting but church growth was slow. I went there with a vision of growing and becoming a thriving church. We had a few folks join, our daughter decided to come with her children. But our son wanted to stay back at the church in Laporte, which was fine with us.

We were getting to know our folks, one of our deacons had knee replacement surgery, and we visited him several times. Debra became the music director, as the lady we had leading music thought she was moving off. Debra was doing a very good job of it and keeping the records as Sunday school director.

In June, we went to San Antonio for our anniversary and went back to my favorite Texas steakhouse. We rode the boats on the river walk and drove up to San Marcos. Then back home as I take off one Sunday in June for our anniversary. But we have been in then ministry at the church.

One Sunday night, as I was getting close to completing a study, I ask the members what they would like for me to teach. Well, one of my deacons asked if I would teach through Revelation to which I answered yes and asked that I would start in two weeks. We begin the series in the study and I was teaching it in depth.

Debra made the comment that this was more in depth than she had ever heard Revelation taught and I needed to publish it in book form. So I decided to see how the publishing process would work. I searched through several and begin to look into pricing. But I wasn't going to make Revelation the first book, not in experimenting with the process. So I sent them another manuscript and paid my fees for publishing. *The Purpose of the Church and Its Members/A Spiritual Life* was born. I sent it to the publishers in October of 2014.

I was working in the North Office for my company and it was too far to drive to Dayton for Wednesday night services. I arrived at the church in LaPorte for Wednesday night services and was feeling really bad and hurting. Debra took one look at me and knew something was wrong. She finally decided to take me to the emergency room and I acquiesced. We arrived, and I was having a hard time breathing and catching my breath. My blood pressure was high, but I was also having PVCs (premature ventricular contractions) as well as congestive heart failure.

Well, they were able to get it straight with me being on oxygen and getting the fluid off of me. But the ER doctor insisted I go see a cardiologist and gave me a doctor's name. That I must go see the next day. Next day, I was seeing that doctor. He said he felt there wasn't anything wrong, but he would run a few test. I didn't like his answer nor his attitude and decided not to go back and see him. A friend from church in Laporte gave the name and number of a cardiologist in the Houston Medical Center. I called and made an appointment with him.

After I saw him for the initial visit and wearing a halter monitor, he definitely felt something was wrong. Ten thousand premature beats in a twenty-four-hour period. That with the congestive heart failure was enough for him to schedule a heart cath. It was scheduled for the second week in November but that wouldn't be made. I made it home from work on a Wednesday, October 28, 2014. Feeling bad yet again. A call to the doctor and he advised we make it to the emergency room at the hospital downtown if possible. Debra drove me, and we found our way to the hospital.

They admitted me for observation overnight, I thought. Boy was I wrong. A series of tests on Thursday, more on Friday, and I needed out for church on Sunday. Saturday rolled around and more testing. But we thought, well that was the final determining test so I should be getting out that evening. It was nearing 7:00 p.m. on Saturday still no discharge and the doctor hadn't come in yet. We made a call to our head deacon, and Debra and his wife along with him decided we would have someone come and preach. I called a friend of mine and he agreed to fill in.

The doctor finally came in with news, news we didn't want to hear.

CHAPTER 17

The Testing and Diagnosis

Well, when the doctor came in, the look on his face was not what we wanted to see. They had found something on the lung, and my heart had some scarring. The nodule on the lung resembled three things that could be wrong: first, tuberculosis, but he was fairly sure it wasn't that. Next, it could be lymphoma, which as we all know is cancer and can be fatal; he was going to have an oncologist review it, and he would see me tomorrow. Then the third, he said was something I had never heard of, sarcoidosis! What was that, what caused it, and what was the cure, all those questions coming out of my mouth! He explained a little about it, that it is a chronic condition and has no cure. Then he said we would wait and see what the oncologist felt before going any further. Not the news either of us wanted to hear.

My evangelist friend ended up with a dead battery the next day and couldn't make it for me. But a man who was a former pastor was attending that day and he filled in for me. Debra arrived early in anticipation of the oncologist coming in. Well, he arrived later in the day, and he felt from what he had seen that it was definitely not lymphoma. He went on to say that if it was, he would have referred me to one of his younger colleagues as he was soon retiring. So we were down to this sarcoidosis and whatever it was.

I was discharged from the hospital and allowed to go home. That was November 2, 2014. I didn't feel well enough to work that Monday but made it in on Tuesday. Then church Wednesday night in Laporte. Message was prepared and ready for Sunday morning and I was back in the pulpit that Sunday. I made an appointment with a pulmonologist. She has treated over five hundred cases of sarcoidosis. They also had me make an appointment with an electrophysiologist to check the electrical impulses to the heart. Debra still believes she nearly lost me that first night if I hadn't gone to the ER.

After visits to the doctors, more testing was scheduled. A bronchoscopy scoping the lungs in an attempt at obtain a piece of the nodule for a biopsy, the other was an electrophysiology (EP) study. The bronchoscopy required breathing in a mist of medicines designed to be an anesthetic for anaesthetizing the throat and bronchial tubes. Then a scope is inserted into the throat and air passage then into the lungs for pictures and to take a section for biopsy. I wasn't able to breathe as much of the mist as needed but the bronchoscopy was performed, but the nodule was on the outside of the lung and a biopsy couldn't be obtained.

My pulmonologist didn't want to go to the next test for a biopsy if she could avoid it. There were some spots on my arm and she wanted a biopsy performed on them, I made an appointment with a dermatologist and the results were not sarcoidosis for them. While all the dermatology work was being performed the EP study was scheduled. Mom wanted to come down for this one, but we didn't think that was necessary. We arrived for the EP study, and I was prepared for the test. The doctor said from the pictures the heart scarring wasn't too bad and he did not anticipate having to implant a defibrillator. This test is a little similar to a heart cauterization, except they insert the device into a vein rather than an artery. They then begin to send electoral impulses into the heart at different points and see how the heart responds. They had me on a drip and sedated but not to where I didn't know what was occurring. Their instruction was lay still and don't get off the table. I was hearing everything that was happening and then it happened. They must have hit the spot where the scarring was because I woke up stiff and my leg were shaking. The nurses screamed, "Stay on the table," and the doctor comes over and says with a funny look on his face, "Are you okay?"

To which I said, "I think so, what happened?"

To which he said, "You passed out." Then the news a defibrillator would need to be implanted and he had other tests, so could his partner come and install the device and I said yes.

Meanwhile, he left me and went to talk to Debra. She said from the look on his face, she thought she had lost me. He explained the situation and what was happening with the defibrillator being inserted, and I would need to spend a night in the hospital.

Upon receiving the results of the skin biopsy and not sarcoid, the final test was scheduled. It was now February 2014, the final test for her to ensure it was sarcoid or lymphoma was a mediastinoscopy with biopsy which is a procedure in which a lighted instrument (mediastinoscope) is inserted in the space in the chest between the lungs (mediastinum). Tissue is taken (biopsy) from any unusual growth or lymph nodes. A very detailed test so it was scheduled.

I went to the hospital for this test as an outpatient. Mom came down for this one with them going into the chest cavity; there are dangers with this one. The day it was scheduled arrived and we sat all day, finally, the doctor who would perform this test came out, it was about 4:30 p.m. I hadn't eaten anything since midnight, he had just completed several, but the last one had taken more time than they had anticipated. He wanted to know if I would come back the next day early and he would ensure I was the very first patient taken and I agreed. While we had been sitting all day in a waiting area, there was a man who was wearing a paper mask over his nose and mouth. Mom had left to get something to drink and Debra begin to talk with this man's wife. He had sarcoid and was there for a follow up after double lung transplants due to the sarcoid.

Next day, we arrived at the time scheduled, and as promised, they took me right in. I had five picks, as they call them, inserted three in one arm, two in the other. One in the wrist where the pulse is located. My neck was prepared for the incision, and I was finally taken back and sedated. Once completed, I awoke in recovery and all they said had gone well.

The next day, my EP cardiologist office called my defibrillator had sent a signal of an incident the day before. Many during the procedure my heart either stopped or the rhythm had drastically been altered. Debra says a third time, she feels she nearly lost me.

The results finally came and my appointment with the pulmonologist was set. It was sarcoid and high doses of prednisone was the only treatment. I was started on it with the hope remission would follow. From February to November, I was on prednisone and the doses were reduced periodically through treatment and eventually weaned off. Remission had come and that was good news for us. Thanksgiving was really a time to be thankful this year.

I had researched sarcoid and gleaned information from all the articles I could find. Looking at the systems plus the effects it can produce I begin family research. Since I had some family from the Scandinavian areas and then the Ferguson's is Scottish. The disease is ten to seventeen times more common in African-Americans than in Caucasians. People of Scandinavian, German, Irish, or Puerto Rican origin are also more prone to the disease. Coker's and Holders I had heard were Irish although the Holder's might be considered German.

All those genes made me very susceptible to sarcoid. Further research showed congestive heart failure is one of the symptoms of sarcoid. Dad most likely died at sixty-two-plus years from heart-related cause, then his dad from lung-related problems and then there was G-Grandmother Carrie who had been a Ferguson. I was able to obtain a copy of her death certificate. She died of congestive heart failure and high arterial pressure, I told my pulmonologist about this and she said that very likely this was the line that carried the genetics for sarcoid.

Christmas and New Year came and 2015 was upon us. 2013 and 2014 had been major year's healthwise. Debra too had been having problems with various things. Had test run for many things and was still not feeling that well. As 2015 began, our journey was not too eventful although at the end of 2014, our daughter's ex-boyfriend from her high school years had come back into her life. He came to the house to visit, and we had a large enough place that he slept on the couch and seemed to stay. Then he left to try and get his affairs taken care of before he would come back into her life.

He did spend thanksgiving and Christmas with us. Then left for his soon to be ex, and then when that didn't work out and she left him for another guy, he came back to our daughter who welcomed him with open arms.

They began to plan a wedding and life together. He was heading home one night and had an accident on his motorcycle. Everything seemed to be okay, but he spent a few days in the hospital and the person he was in the accident with paid for everything. He began his search for a job and their plans were in the works. Overall, those two years saw God watching over us as we continued "Our Adventurous Journey."

CHAPTER 18

New Year and New Additions

As 2015 began, Debra and I planned a trip for our fortieth wedding anniversary. A trip to where and what type. She wanted to take a cruise or something on that scale. I began to search the internet and see what we could do.

The church was growing a little as the year began with our daughter and her children joining. I hadn't finished the Revelation study on Sunday night, but in late December, I had sent a copy of the introduction and first chapter of a book that would become the series of four on Revelation, *The Snatching Away* was completed, but I would need to have it published. I sent those portions to a few publishing companies and began to receive answers on cost back, then I received this from my current publisher; from the director of book acquisitions, she stated, "This is wonderful. Would you want to consider our publisher for life option?"

Debra and I discussed the cost and the opportunity and we decided that this would be a great deal. I signed the contract and began to pay for the publishing. I also sent the book through and now had two in publishing mode. The next two were being compiled, but the fourth would not be ready until I completed the study.

On January 13, 2015, I received an email that *The Snatching Away of the Bride* had been assigned a project manager it was on its way.

At the same time, I had the second book ready, *Beginning of Earth's Redemption*, and I forwarded that manuscript to the publishers. Then I was informed it would be delayed until the second book had been submitted to marketing. All in all, I was working on several more books.

I had begun to teach on Wednesday night at the church in 2014 and had placed a box in the fellowship hall where we met and had the members drop questions into the box. I would then form a message around those questions. It is ready to go to the publishers and may be sent even after this one.

2015 our daughter and her now fiancé began the planning stages for the wedding. Our son had joined our church and was started ensuring the PA system was working correctly. A young lady begin to attend, and well, God must have had it planned for them to get together. They too became a couple, and well, more wedding plans were now being made. Two weddings in the same year. She had two boys and they were not in her care and custody at the time, but she was working toward getting them back; circumstances in her life had led to a bad situation.

In mid-January, I had booked a cruise for our anniversary; we would sail from Galveston to Cozumel and back. Those plans were set and firm; no wedding could take place around that time. My son and his fiancée were talking about an October or even December. Our daughter and her fiancé were talking June or July, circumstances dictated interfered, and they settled on mid-September.

Then they had to settle on where: some suggested our church, maybe the church we had attended in LaPorte, while other ideas were in a hotel meeting room. She would need a dress and of course who would stand up with her. She decided her future sister-in-law would be her maid of honor and her daughter would be the flower girl. Since I was performing the wedding, her oldest son would walk her down the aisle and give her away. They found a hotel package, and it was close to the house. The dress was found and things were taking shape.

June came and our cruise for out fortieth anniversary. We packed and our son and his fiancée drove us to the dock for us to embark on our trip. We received express check-in with my health situation I was in a wheelchair. We carried on our luggage with it all in my lap as we were taken to our cabin.

The ship sailed promptly at 4:00 p.m. and we were at sea. We went to dinner on our deck which was the Liddo Deck where all but the main dining rooms are, the pool was on that too. We walked the deck and just talked, then I found the itinerary pamphlet and we saw what was going on in different places. We decided to go check some things out.

Debra wanted to play BINGO, then there were shows, one was similar to the newlywed game, another was a tribute to America. Then there were the movies on the big screen and of course music on the Liddo Deck with the pools and the DJ.

We wanted to go on a shore excursion and couldn't quite decide on the non-stressful ones, but we found a tour of the island. Taken to a chocolate factory and see how the coco beans are harvested dried and ground. Then how the other ingredients are added and then a taste of the still liquefied chocolate on a spoon. Then to a shop to purchase 85 percent chocolate bars.

From there, we went to a little village where the oldest Catholic church on the Yucatan area can be found and an ancient Mayan temple right next to it. The people there can harvest coral and made necklace sets and sold them there, a lot less expensive that the shops at the port.

The final portion of the tour was to be to the virgin side of the island that is Cozumel. We booked that excursion, and upon arriving in Cozumel, the rain was torrential as Tropical Storm Bill was forming.

As we disembarked from the ship, the cruise line crew was distributing ponchos for everyone. Many of the excursions were cancelled but not ours at least not to start. We toured the chocolate factory, then went to the village and purchased the necklace sets and toured the tequila factory.

The vehicle we were in had a major roof leak, and the defroster didn't work; we were all asked if we wanted to finish the tour and the majority said no, so we went back to the plaza at the port.

Debra had a coupon for a bracelet, and we picked that up and returned to the ship and waited for the cruise to continue. As we were getting underway, the ship began to list most likely 15 to 20 degrees, the pictures were hanging away from the wall, and the water in the pool was flowing onto the deck; it was a bad list. Debra and I were at the food court, and instead returning to the room across the deck, we entered the elevator to the floor below and walked forward to our room. As we walked the corridor, there were people screaming and panicking on that floor. Eventually, the ship listing was corrected. As we passed some folks during the list, I made the comment we all needed to go the port side and that would straighten us out, they didn't see the humor in that statement.

We dressed for the elegant dinner night and went to dinner in the dining room. The next day, the sun finally burst out and the deck party continued. Soon, we would be back home and off to work and church. A week or two after arriving home, we booked another cruise for Debra's birthday in November, hoping for a little better weather.

As we returned, we received news that our son and his fiancée were thinking of moving the wedding up. She and her mother weren't seeing eye to eye, and they were thinking about October instead of waiting till February. They were trying to decide as our daughter's was approaching quickly, September wasn't that far away. I suggested a double wedding to save time and money, but our daughter wanted no part of a double wedding.

As the middle of August arrived, the tension with our future daughter-in-law and her mother had escalated to the point that she was asked to move out of her mother's home. They set a date for mid-September a week after our daughter's wedding! Now two weddings in the span of a week.

Our son and future daughter-in-law's wedding would be at the church; she had always wanted a church wedding and now would have it. Our son being an Elvis impersonator wanted a Blue Hawaii wedding theme and would even sing the wedding son to her. Debra's sister came to the shower and sprang into action with the décor and planning.

September 12, 2015; arrived and we all got ready, our daughter and party went to the hotel and their room to dress in her wedding gown; a lavender formal dress. Purple shirts on the boys and a purple and white dress for her daughter. I went and purchased a new suit since I was performing two weddings in that week span. I purchased an off white suit with a lavender shirt and fuchsia shirt that way, the suit could be worn for both weddings. Our future daughter-in-law loved the color pink. The wedding went off without a hitch, and we had the grandkids and our son part of the time. He had begun to stay in the travel trailer at the church to be able to drive his fiancé to her many meetings and classes.

They would live in the travel trailer, and we would pay any excess of the light bill to the church. Their wedding was fast approaching. Debra and the future daughter-in-law as well as our daughter went dress hunting. Thrift and resale shops. I even accompanied Debra and them on a few trips. She found a black formal dress that she said she could wear a white shawl with. But they said one last stop. I stayed in the vehicle while they went in and our daughter comes out to get Debra's purse. They had found the perfect dress, and it fit perfectly. Dress was now in hand and two weeks before the wedding. Our future daughter-in-law had sent pictures of the black one and people were thinking that would be her dress and she was going to surprise everyone at the wedding.

Our son was going with white pants and a white shirt with a pink sash around the waist, and Debra's sister had made a shoulder and neck wrap for the bride. All was in place for a September 19 wedding. As the day arrived, we all dressed and arrived at the church. Our son would get dressed in the Sunday school room behind the auditorium while she would dress in the restrooms. Debra's brother-in-law would take pictures and her sister was the consummate wedding planner. The wedding occurred with no mishaps and pictures were taken. Then the reception and they would go out to eat and then come back to the trailer.

They, like Debra and I, would be in church the day after the wedding. They kept that tradition alive. They travelled several times during the week down to the house for things he had going on with

Special Olympics and meetings for her. We now had two additions in our home. She was working hard to get her children back and other issues in her life, but now she had a stable husband and family to help her make the changes she needed.

CHAPTER 19
The Next Part of the Adventure

As Thanksgiving approached and Christmas came with our new additions, Debra and I made plans for our next cruise. This time, we would leave on a Monday and be back on Saturday, only missing a Wednesday night service. This trip we knew how to make our way around on the cruise ship. We took in the shows, and she of course wanted to play bingo. We actually took advantage of the pools on this trip. The seas seemed a little rough especially for Debra.

This time, no major storm as we left Progresso and then arrived at Cozumel again, this time we booked the same excursion and were able to take the tour all the way around the island. Another necklace set, and this time, two charm bracelets for the daughter and daughter-in-law. We had steak in the steak house for her birthday and then had breakfast in the dining room once this time. We met some very nice couples at that breakfast and went back that night for dinner and sat with them too.

When we arrived home, all was going well and Thanksgiving would be coming up in a few days and we would then have Christmas coming. Before the cruise in October, I noticed some bumps coming up on my arm and I was exceptionally tired. An appointment to see my pulmonologist. She saw the nodules and the lung function as well as the tiredness and back on prednisone, the sarcoid was active yet again.

Boarding the ship and then a safety drill. I almost passed out during the safety drill. But they moved me into a lobby area and we continued on the trip. This Thanksgiving and Christmas, I would be battling the sarcoid. During this time, we also received news our daughter-in-law was expecting; our son was going to be a father for the first time at thirty-eight years old.

As she began to work on getting Medicaid and finally approved, she was able to go to the doctor and an ultrasound was performed. Twins and too early to determine their gender. But now, two more grandchildren would be added to our family.

That made us expecting four new people in our home with the daughter-in-law's two older ones and now twins. February came and the nodules were gone on my arm, and I was weaned off of prednisone yet again. Hoping it was for the last time, praying I would stay in remission. Debra and I were talking a cruise for our anniversary and/or her birthday again and/or a trip to her mother's.

We discussed driving to her mother's, but we couldn't go until August. I had book events every month except May. For a cruise in June, we would need to be back for that event. The decision was made to travel to her mom's in North Carolina. But we would drive.

Plans for an additional room in the house to accommodate all the grandchildren and children were being made. We had one spot in the house proper or a room out of one side of the garage. Debra and I even contemplated moving to the downstairs bedroom and giving up the master. But the room addition became the best option, and we would need it anyway.

June came and our anniversary this year, we would stay home and go to a restaurant to eat. I ordered her a snow globe for a present as well as card. We went out and enjoyed our time together, but work was slowing and things again were at a slow pace. I was sent to a field project to ensure all the valves and material would flow in a timely fashion.

The twin boys were born, and we brought them home, the oldest was six pounds, one ounce while the youngest was five pounds, six ounces, both nineteen inches long. Beautiful baby boys and the legacy of the family. The oldest grandson now twelve carries on the name as well, but these are from the only son of my dad. Oh, that Dad was here to enjoy this time with his buddy, my son.

When we found out about the weddings and then approaching birth of these babies I became inspired to write a book about my dad in 2015, he was a great man of God and went through many trials and troubles in his life. *A Christian Father: A Man of Faith* was written and submitted in 2016, it is currently published and available for order.

July flew by as the years seem to be doing as I get older. But I noticed yet again a nodule on my left arm this time. I again was extremely fatigued a trip to the doctor again and back on prednisone, a low dose this time. August came and Debra and I drove to North Carolina. Her mom and stepdad had their home on the market, and while we were there, it sold. We went and saw the new place they would be living. We were going to go to a hoedown, but I got to feeling bad. My arm stiffens and then shakes uncontrollably, I guess I am not getting enough oxygen. Before we left, I picked up an office chair at work and began to wheeze from shortness of breath.

As we left for home, we travelled for about ten hours before stopping and then through the storms in Alabama, Mississippi, and Louisiana that caused the flood waters in Louisiana that year. Again, we reminisced about the trip in 1978 when she was carrying our son. Remembering seeing her grandmother and time spent with her aunts and uncles. We talked of the trip I made in 1971 with Mom and crew to Mississippi. On the way to North Carolina, we went by way of Hattiesburg and wondered about the friends we had made in Richton, trying to recall their names. Remembering the times in the trailer and our daughter's first pair of glasses at eighteen months. How she rustled the leaves as if she had never seen them clearly before. All in all, it was a great trip.

God has me in his plans and he knows what is happening and going to happen. I followed the doctor's orders and kept praying for His will to be accomplished through it all. I was still working, preaching, writing, and doing everything I could with the family.

Mom sold her place in Arkansas. Both our parents are started new chapters in their lives. Mom called asking me to find her and apartment. I made some calls and found her a two-bedroom close to our home. Debra and I flew to Arkansas and drove a U-haul truck down with her belongings and her car in tow.

She had been having some health issues and I made her appointments to get things checked out. We went to the appointments and then testing. Prescriptions were written, and Mom is now on her new journey.

CHAPTER 20

Major Decisions and Changes

After arriving back home from North Carolina, the first Sunday, I brought my message and all seemed well. As we arrived at church for Wednesday night service, I noticed several vehicles of members who seldom attended Wednesday night services. I turned to Debra commenting about the vehicles and said something is up.

Entering the fellowship hall and saw several people that we were surprised at being there. The deacon immediately made a statement, "We're not having a preaching service, we're having a gripe session." After prayer, he stated, "We have a list of things we want to discuss." Each one was of course something they saw wrong in what we as pastor and family were doing. After each one was stated, I said it had been taken of, but each was not to their liking, with the exception of one item that really needed discussion. Things got tense toward the end, and we had prayer and left.

By Sunday, I decided to announce my resignation. Instead of a sermon, I read the document. The church asked if it was final, and I said they could vote to accept or reject it. It was announced that day, and the following Wednesday, a special called meeting that would be the next Sunday to discuss and vote.

Sunday arrived fast and almost all members were there. I preached a message and we went into the called business meeting. The purpose and the list of seven grievances was discussed. A secret ballot vote followed the discussion. A unanimous vote was cast for me to continue as pastor. The deacon and a few others didn't attend. God was at work.

I continued pastoring the church as well as working through the end of the year on my job. My boss called me into his office and told me they were going to lay me off. I said since my illness was affecting me, why not go on disability. First short term and then long term. That was put into motion.

I had enough vacation time and sick leave to carry me through the year and into 2017. I started the Christmas holidays and never went back to work. My final day to actually be employed was in April of 2017. Short-term disability insurance had begun and long term started shortly thereafter. I was also able to get SSDI started for myself.

We booked another cruise for August 2017, this time seven days, three port of calls. But that cruise would have to be cancelled as Harvey was brewing out in the Gulf of Mexico and would land on the upper Texas Coast. We were staying in, and all thirteen of us found ways to stay entertained.

We booked another cruise, this being a seven-day to three different ports than the one cancelled. This would leave in November just after Debra's birthday. A birthday cruise for her and right before Thanksgiving. Jamaica, Cayman Islands, Cozumel, and back to Galveston. We had a fun time on that cruise and the kids kept things in control. We booked the same excursion on Cozumel as well as an excursion on at Jamaica and then Cayman Islands where we visited a place called Hell.

I resigned the church at the end of 2017. We had seen many other problems occurring there. It was time to leave after four years. We left, having made several new friends in the Lord. Therefore, 2018 would begin with me out of work and now not pastoring. Time to stay home for a while see what the Lord had planned.

Things at home had started to have a few problems as well. Not with Debra and I, but with the other family members. Our son and his wife were having problems. Things escalated and she left our home with the four boys. She kept the twins from their daddy for eight long months. Visitation would be set, and she would have a reason not to come. We finally retained a lawyer for him and were able to go to court and have custody orders established.

The Lord was at work as usual, and our son was given custodial conservatorship. We had papers in hand and, having found where she was living, tried to have our daughter-in-law turn the twins over as per the orders. She refused and our lawyer served her with a writ of habeas corpus. In June, we went to court; the twins were awarded to him that very day we left the courthouse, babies in our care.

Our daughter-in-law decided to return to our home in September of that 2018. Her and the two older boys. But things weren't a bed of roses for them like she assumed it should be. Debra and I booked another trip. We would not leave from Galveston but decided to embark from Miami on a seven-day cruise. Miami to Cayman Islands, then Isle of Roatan, Belize then Cozumel, and back to Miami. We went on excursion in Isla of Roatan and Cozumel. Isle of Roatan, we went to a botanical farm of sorts. Made chocolate and then had a cultural lunch of the country's favorite chicken dish. Cozumel was a glass bottom boat tour.

Instead of flying straight home, we flew to North Carolina to visit Debra's mom and stepdad. Then fly back home in time for Thanksgiving. We were attending a new church and I was asked to supply for a few services in December. We made it to the holidays and New Year without much trouble.

As 2019 started without much trouble, they weren't getting along. She was having some personal issues and health problems. She finally decided to leave yet again in April 2019. She made a decision that would not work out well for her. She decided to leave and move in with her ex-boyfriend. Violating the custody orders, thinking they were no longer in effect, twins with her. Our lawyer filed for another writ of habeas corpus. Again, on our court date in May, the twins were awarded back to our son's custody a second time. God was at work as we trusted in Him and our prayers were answered.

We had booked another birthday cruise for Debra in 2019. This one would embark from Tampa to Cayman Islands, then Cozumel and back to Tampa. We didn't take an excursion on the Cayman Island portion this time. In Cozumel, we went on an interesting excursion with a tour of a museum of sorts.

Before leaving, Debra would need shoulder surgery. The tendon in her shoulder was popping out of socket. The doctor would put a screw in the shoulder and reattach the tendon. While he was performing the surgery, frozen shoulder was found and the doctor scrapped that out.

One Saturday in October, the Lord revealed a plan for Debra and I. after spending several months sending resumes to churches. Then Debra saying please don't send anymore as I was supplying and teaching at the new church, I received a phone call. This was on a Saturday morning. The director of missions in an association of churches was on the phone.

"Could I supply for a church? Sure, when do you need me?" I asked.

"Sunday," he said.

"Sure, I would supply."

The church was seventy-five miles from home.

I filled in that Sunday, and they asked if I could come back the next Sunday. I said I would, and it continued that way each Sunday. We told them when we could and made it that way till the end of the year.

After arriving home and before Thanksgiving, Debra would have a knee replacement. We spent Thanksgiving and Christmas with her laid-up form that surgery. We missed a few Sundays but were back at the church supplying a few Sundays in December.

The doctors had performed several procedures on me during this time too. I am now carrying a medical pillow that reads the pressures in my pulmonary artery. Every morning, I lay on the pillow and it reads my pressures. This accompanied us on the cruise.

With all of these things occurring, our son also needed back surgery and therapy following. I am still suffering from CHF, and they are wanting to do more procedures. But I put those off to care for Debra, our son, and the twins.

When the holidays season arrived, our daughter and her husband made a decision. They were moving to the country on his dad's property. Our son-in-law had a house there, and they felt the children would do better in school.

As 2020 started out with me taking care of those down and the twins. While that was happening, the doctor ordered test for me. X-rays for this, scans for that. Physical therapy for Debra and our son. Chasing the rambunctious twins. Going and checking on Mom.

CHAPTER 21

What's Next on This Journey?

As for the new church, I had asked their plans and what they were wanting. They had said wait till the New Year and we'll let you know. Well, they asked me the Sunday after the New Year if I would be their pastor. I said let Debra and I discuss it and pray about it. I asked the next Sunday if we could meet with them and discuss what they wanted. It ended with me becoming their pastor.

I had found that their pastor had passed away in 2017. They had called a man to be their pastor and he had accepted. On a specific Sunday, he had come to let them know his health was not going to allow him to continue. While in the pulpit, he passed out and hadn't been able to fill the pulpit since.

Then March 2020 arrived, we all know the Covid-19 pandemic arrived in the USA. On March 1, we conducted a pastor installation service. Then another service and orders came down: stay home and work safe.

We've not been to the church in several weeks, but we've learned to adapt. Facebook live streaming services. Then upload to YouTube and reach people via the airwaves. Now re-releasing this book and what it may hold.

What is coming next on this adventurous journey, only God knows. We have tests and possibly other things coming for my health. Debra's still working through the knee and is improving every week. Our son and his back need some help, but that won't happen until the Covid-19 pandemic has run its course.

The twins will turn four this year and school will begin for them. New adventures for their lives and for the other three grand-children. A family reunion was planned for March but had to be postponed. Now it is scheduled for the fall of this year.

Covid-19 has many people's plans on hold. Many are panicking, hoarding and many other things. A friend of mine has been battling for nearly two weeks and has just begun to start a healing process.

It has been an adventurous journey for us as we continue to live it. God has worked so much out in our lives over the years. Especially these last three years. Seeing Him work through our son's situation. His answering prayer upon prayer for the welfare of our twin grandsons.

How I had stopped looking to pastor again and yet God opened a door wide open. Saying go and trust me to guide you. He has a plan and He will work it out. As we have learned and are still learning to TRUST Him through it all and in it all. We will continue to seek God's will and guidance for Our Life's Adventurous Journey.

CONCLUSION

The only thing sure is God is on the throne and at work and He has plans for our lives. As we are now in retirement, it was hard to see retirement ever occurring. God caused all things to work for His good in our lives. We just need to continue trusting Him as best we can, salvation is sure no matter what we are saved.

My day is coming; the nodule disappeared and I seem to have stayed in remission. I know God holds me in His hand, and His will is going to be accomplished.

Salvation comes to all who by faith receive Christ and His efficacious death on the cross. My quiver is full of grandchildren, and I pray that they will all come to Christ to fulfill my dad's legacy.

As I wrote this book, my hope is that I have fulfilled what God had for me to accomplish and that I will continue to do just that. That as a son, brother, husband, father, and grandfather, I have truly made a difference in the lives of all those around me. To them all, I say I love you all very much, and maybe that is enough to say, I succeeded at one thing in my life. I hope I became the man Dad expected me to be. Debra's been a faithful and loving wife. A source of help and support as we walk through this life together. For however long we have left, our love is strong and our faith stronger. We still have things come up in our lives that need to be worked through and out, but all things are possible through faith and with God's guidance. Our final destination of Our Adventurous Journey has not been reached, but heaven is our home and we will be there soon!

CPSIA information can be obtained
at www.ICGtesting.com
Printed in the USA
BVHW071047101120
592962BV00002B/368